D1536323

Growing Up
in an
Amish-Jewish Cult

Book Three

Deliverance

Patricia Hochstetler

Growing Up
in an
Amish-Jewish Cult

Book Three
Deliverance

BAKER TRITTIN PRESS
Winona Lake, Indiana

Copyright © 2008 Patricia Hochstetler

All rights reserved. No part of this publication may be reproduced or transmitted in any form or by any means, electronic or mechanical including photocopying, recording, or by any information storage and retrieval system, without written permission of the publisher.

Growing Up in an Amish-Jewish Cult / Book Three, Deliverance
By Patricia Hochstetler

Printed in the United States of America
Cover Design: Paul S. Trittin
Back Cover Photos: Mike Albin
Published by Baker Trittin Press
P.O. Box 277
Winona Lake, Indiana 46590

To order additional copies please call (574) 269-6100
or email info@btconcepts.com
http://www.bakertrittinpress.com

Publishers Cataloging-Publication Data
Patricia Hochstetler, 1948-
        Growing Up in an Amish-Jewish Cult/ Book Three,
        Deliverance
        Patricia Hochstetler - Winona Lake, Indiana
        Baker Trittin Press, 2007

                p.   cm.

Library of Congress Control Number: 2008922281
ISBN 10: 0-9787316-6-2
ISBN 13: 978-0-9787316-6-3
        1. Autobiography 2. Religious 3. Christian
        I. Title   II. Growing Up in an Amish-Jewish Cult /
        Book Three, Deliverance
BIO18000

Acknowledgements

The following individuals have played essential roles in the *Growing Up in an Amish-Jewish Cult* trilogy. This book, and the previous two books, are written to give others hope and to help them see the power of God.

I must acknowledge all of the Lael Colony members who shared their recollections of the life we survived. May God bless you! Also to my grandmother, the late Bertha Long, who God used as an instrument in my deliverance.

These books were written with the patience and support of my husband, Ezra, my children and grandchildren, and also friends and church family.

My gratitude goes to all my mentors, transcribers, college professors, writer's club members, editors, reviewers, website assistants, conference educators, prayer partners, and all those who contributed in any way to this book and trilogy.

Through the masterful hand of Dr. Marvin Baker's editing and Paul Trittin's keen publishing abilities this series is layed out according to God's plan and timing. Thank you for all your efforts, guidance, and encouragement in making this a reality to show the danger of cults and the power of God's deliverance.

I also humbly thank the public, especially the people of my background, the Amish, for their support of my first two books, *Delusion* and *Deception*, which has far exceeded my expectations.

Mostly, I must thank and praise the Lord Jesus Christ, my Master and Savior, who with love, mercy, and grace spared my life and delivered me from despair to salvation.

Table of Contents

Preface

After ten years of interviews with family and friends, Patricia Hochstetler was finally ready to organize her thoughts and emotions in preparation to tell her strange experiences to her husband, children, grandchildren, and friends. Though she had little or no formal education of any kind, she was allowed to enroll in writing classes at a local college and a university. At one point she asked a trusted writing professor to write her story for her. He knew that no one could write it as she could and encouraged her to continue studying so she would be enabled to write it herself.

He obviously wasn't expecting her to write a classic tale in the prosaic language of a highly educated wordsmith. He assumed she would write in simple language full of the wonderment, simple faith, and fear of the child she was when her life was in bondage to a unique belief system that she now identifies as an Amish-Jewish cult. That title is peculiar not in that it was a hybrid between Old Testament Judaism and Amish traditions, but because those who finally broke away, carry few vestiges of either Jewishness or Amishness in their present lives.

I hope you have been able to read the first two books in her trilogy. In them she shares the unbelievable account of her entry into the isolated community of Lael Colony when she was only four and then of her difficult life from the age of six to sixteen picking cotton in the fields of Mississippi for twelve hours a day. Such a life would totally change most of us. How many would have survived still carrying within us a desperate hunger for God?

That has been the beauty of working with Patricia. In her I have seen an uncomplicated and simple faith in her Savior in spite of twelve years of uncompromising hardship and psychological abuse. She carries within her a strength that can only be born of a faith unfathomably greater than the obstacles she endured.

It is here that I must warn you of the content of her tale as you will read it in *Deliverance*. It is not a resounding message of victory over oppression and spiritual darkness as I had thought it would be as we first spoke with her of a need to convey her story in three separate volumes. Far from it. What you will discover is that it is often easier for a person to be removed from a cult than it is to remove the cult from within the person liberated.

Patricia so clearly points this out as she recalls her teenage years. This feat takes time, often years to purge from a wounded life. She demonstrates that it can only be achieved through our openness to the working of the Holy Spirit and the power of Jesus Christ. The blind cannot heal themselves.

As you read *Deliverance,* I am sure your heart will be broken as was mine, but I pray you will also rejoice with Patricia for the matchless love of God. His grace is truly greater than all our sin, and much greater still than all our attempts to do good works.

Paul S. Trittin
Publisher

Chapter 1

My First Day in a New World

We left behind all that I had known. God had spared our lives, and now a whole new world that I was not prepared to face was passing before my eyes.

Thursday, June 11, 1964, was extremely hot and muggy. Hours spent riding in a stuffed station wagon did not soften the reality that I was – we were – forced to leave everything our family had hoped for – a spiritual refuge.

After endless hours we stopped in front of a house that looked totally unfamiliar to me. My English Grandma Long, Dad's Mom, told us we were in Elkhart, Indiana, and this was her house. I was born in this town 16 years earlier.

Uncle Carl, our driver, Grandma, Mom, my brother, sister, Shag – our dog, and I piled out of Uncle Carl's station wagon that was packed to the roof with our belongings. We were thankful to have our feet planted firmly on the ground after our long and turbulent journey from Clarksdale, Mississippi. It was hard to accept that this was supposed to replace the isolated Lael Colony where I grew up.

Happy to be out of the stuffed car and cramped position, I found the unknown pounding at my thoughts. What would I face next? What would we all face in this foreign, noisy world after leaving our quiet colony? At least the outside of Grandma's house appealed to me. It was a spacious looking bungalow covered with brown and tan shingles that looked much like bricks. It even had an unbelievable screened-in front porch and a high solid stone foundation.

The moment Shag hopped out of the car he was happy, curious, and exploring everything. He gave his typical bird dog hunting stance. His white, feathered tail pointed straight out and one front, white paw was raised. His black ears were up and at alert. A distinct white mark separated his two, big, brown eyes that beamed at every site. A platter-size, black spot on his left shoulder and a saucer size one in the middle of his back stood out on his snow white, furry coat. Soon we three children walked sheepishly beside Shag and explored the backyard.

"Wait a minute," Grandma called. "You need to know that dogs can't run loose in the city."

"Why is that, Grandma?" Fred asked.

It was a surprise to us. Shag had never had a collar or chain on his neck.

"Well, that's the city rules. Dogs running loose in the city can cause problems," she explained. We locked Shag in the garage and fed him before we went into the house. As the cars passed on the busy street, the people stared at us, and I was relieved to go into the house.

We entered the back door into Grandma's kitchen, and I quickly noticed her fancy red clock. How worldly everything looked! *Oh, Grandma's clock is red,* I thought, and then immediately *red is bad* flashed through my mind. *Stop-sign red is of the devil, hell fire, and evil,* I thought as I remembered The Elder's teaching. I had learned about stop-sign red as we traveled to Indiana.

Below the clock was a rectangular box. When they turned it on, I couldn't understand this one any better than the one in the car. The scrambled voices sounded like a confused rumble. My sensitive ears felt battered with this noise the worldly people claimed was "words with a beat." It sounded like a mix of hundreds of cackling hens and a fox. I couldn't understand the words or whatever they said was beating. They said this was called music! I added that to my new vocabulary.

Pictures hung on the walls. Some were even of people. *Unfastanlich!* (Unbelievable!) These false images in the likeness of God were forbidden for us. Flowers planted by people instead of God were everywhere in and out of the house.

According to The Elder this was another sign of worldly sin. Grandma showed us – and encouraged us – to use her inside toilet with water that swirled around and disappeared just like those amazing ones we saw earlier that day. I was fascinated by its magical operation. This phenomenon seemed good and odorless. It was nothing like the *hizley* (outhouse) we always used where the odor was continuous and strong enough to make a fly vomit. A fancy, soft, white paper they called toilet paper—too nice for what they said to use it for—all rolled up, hung on a holder fastened to the wall. This was so different from the old catalogs, leaves, and corncobs we used. I heard my first whisper of doubt as I wondered why The Elder said everything outside of Lael Colony was evil. I liked this clean idea and couldn't see why it was wrong.

With a twist of the wrist Grandma instantly lit her stove. It was hard to believe! She didn't use wood or kerosene like we did in the colony. Before long the unknown aroma of cooking beef and noodles filled the air I was curious about this foreign bone-colored ribbon-type food Grandma called noodles. The beef was also something unfamiliar to us. The meat we ate in the colony was mostly chicken and pigeon. The greenish, white, layered ball Grandma called head lettuce was fascinating because we never saw a round head like that before. We ate leaf lettuce from our garden but only in the spring when it was in season. This meal with all the trimmings was quickly prepared. Amazing! The small drop leaf table was separated in the middle and two boards were speedily inserted. It was large enough for all of us!

We sat at Grandma's table ready to eat when she unexpectedly prayed, "Thank you, God, for allowing me to find my son and his family. Thank you for my grandchildren who I have found to be alive. . . ." Choking back tears she continued, ". . . and still on this earth. Thank you for bringing us all back safely to Indiana. Thank you for answering my many prayers and making my dreams come true. Lord, please be with my boy, Clarence, in the hospital, and bless each one around this table, and bless this food for its intended use. Amen."

This was the first time I had heard a woman cry or pray. It seemed scary. And Grandma prayed without a head covering! I was sure this was contrary to the Bible and I was positive it was contrary to what I was taught. A woman praying out loud? That's wrong too. That's only for men! Will God answer her prayers, or will He even hear them?

Grandma seemed stressed yet happy when she said, "Don't be shy now. Eat."

We couldn't eat anything against our dietary laws like pork. I didn't plan to eat a bite of anything unless I knew for sure that it was kosher. Being too shy to ask, I decided not to eat. Then Mom silently signaled with a nod and finger point that we should eat mashed potatoes and biscuits that she helped prepare and declared dietary safe. However I had no appetite and felt half-sick. Knots throbbed in my throat and stomach. I ate a few bites of mashed potatoes and drank the unusual, tasteless water. When the meal was over, we washed dishes in Grandma's strange, fancy sink and cleaned the kitchen.

"I'm going to call Marie. Do you remember Clarence's sister?" Grandma asked Mom.

"Doesn't she have a daughter, Connie?" Grandma nodded and Mom kept talking. "I baby-sat for her before we moved to the colony."

Later that day they came to Grandma's house to visit us, but they seemed like strangers. I thought they acted strange too. They stared at us. It was hard for me to understand them. I didn't know what to say and blushed every time they spoke to me. They looked shamefully more than half-naked to me, and I was embarrassed to look at all the bare skin they showed.

My aunt had fewer clothes covering her entire body than I had on in only my underclothes. Of course my underpants were ankle-length and my slip and dress were about a half-inch from the floor.

Soon my aunt said to me, "Where did you get those long, thick, hot-looking clothes? I knew you wore long dresses, but I thought they would look and be more like the Amish, shorter, thinner, and more comfortable. Are your clothes cult uniforms or what?"

Speechless, I could tell she viewed me as a freak and as foreign as I did her.

"Why don't you take some of those long, heavy clothes off? Aren't you hot with long sleeves and a thick floor length dress on?" Aunt Marie asked.

"No, I'm comfortable in my clothes."

I wouldn't have taken anything off even if it was 100 degrees and I was wringing wet with sweat like I often was in the cotton fields. I had on what I was used to wearing every day of my life. They felt good, and I was well covered like I was taught I should be. My face and hands were the only skin that could show. If more was exposed, I would not have felt presentable.

I felt very uneasy with these people sizing me up, and I had nothing to say to them. Since we were taught everyone outside our colony were heathens, I felt surrounded by many devils waiting to snare me. It was frightening. I wanted to hide. I felt language impaired and conversationally lost listening to them. They used slang words and joked, and I had never heard either before. I certainly didn't fit in this environment of jolly jokes and laughter. I felt as stiff as a corpse. Mummified, I waited for them to leave.

When they did leave, I continued to feel fearful, stiff, emotionless, and stunned.

Many years later I asked Aunt Marie what she thought when she first saw us after we returned to Indiana. She responded, "I thought, 'Those poor children! They are handicaps in society. What will ever happen to them? How in this world will they make it?' I felt sorry for all of you, but I didn't know what to do or say."

I could identify with her questions. I, too, wondered how we would make it, but our perspectives were poles apart. She wondered how we would survive in her world. I wondered how I could survive here among all these heathen and worldly people. I would not tell any more to people than what they could pump out of me.

Ever since we had left Mississippi, my face was swollen from badly infected teeth, but I wouldn't tell anyone. Mom warned me that the worldly people took painkillers — whatever that was — and if they knew how much I hurt they might insist I take them too. I never had taken any pills before and wouldn't take them now because all medicine was against our rules. God is the Healer, and if He chose to heal me, He would. I was determined to wait on Him and didn't want anyone forcing anything on me that was evil or sinful.

Other relatives we didn't know visited that first day. Finally everyone left except Uncle Carl who lived with Grandma. Evening came and Grandma with the flip of a finger turned on extremely bright lights in her kitchen and then all over the house. I didn't understand how this was possible. What kept the house from catching on fire? I was convinced that when our kerosene lamps were lit we were much safer because we knew the fire was confined and not hanging from the ceiling and walls. Grandma tried to explain how this marvel, electricity, worked.

That evening she encouraged everyone to take a bath or shower before getting into her clean beds. Off from the kitchen, between the back door and kitchen table, a door led to a small bathroom. It was filled with the most foreign things that I had never imagined existed. There were perfumes, powders, hair gadgets, spraying cans, medicines, and band-aids. The mixture of odors filled the air. All across the back wall was an unusual, huge, long, white shinny thing Grandma called a bathtub. A long, floral curtain draped down over one side. The only kind of tubs I knew were the round galvanized ones we put water and scrub boards in. We scrubbed our dirty clothes by hand in them on wash day. When we were small, we took baths in them too.

At one end on the wall high above Grandma's bathtub hung a funny sprayer thing she called a shower. My facial expression revealed my lack of understanding.

"The water will sprinkle over you like rain," Grandma

explained. Seeing my uncertainty, she continued her instructions.

"Stand under the sprinkler and get wet all over. Then wash with the soap. Rinse and use the towel to dry off."

I was not totally convinced. But I was more concerned about the spiritual issue. Was it sinful or wrong to have water raining down over you while standing naked in an oversize tub? I wasn't sure.

"It's easier and quicker than a bath. You should try it," Grandma encouraged.

She talked me into trying the shower and laid out a towel and wash cloth with a plastic bubble on top.

"What's that," I asked as I pointed to the plastic object.

"That's a shower cap. You won't get all of that hair wet if you wear it," Grandma replied.

Mom sitting at the kitchen table called to assure me, "It's okay! You can use it as a head covering."

The first thing I thought of was that I could even pray in the shower's rain and God would hear my prayers. This was great! I always liked walking in the rain, and now I could stand still in it. This was so different than the sponge bathes we've taken for the past ten years.

"When you're undressed and ready to get in the shower, I'll turn it on for you." Grandma offered.

Mom, knowing there wasn't a chance of that happening, interrupted, "No, she's too modest and won't undress first."

Puzzled, Grandma turned the shower water on first and showed me how to turn it off. She went out the door saying, "Now hurry, so we won't run out of hot water."

I didn't have a clue what she meant other than I was to undress and wash fast. Going in this tiny room and taking off all my clothes without a lock on the door was frightening. There were people outside the door sitting around the kitchen table talking.

Mom sensed my uncertainty and said, "I'll sit in this chair nearest the bathroom door and watch to make sure nobody goes in."

This was still very hard for me to do. Nobody had seen my naked body and nobody was going to now! I stood right inside the door to undress so if someone opened it, I served as a big door stop and a double guard until the moment I could dash into the raining shower.

As I rushed, I suddenly saw a mirror above the sink. *What am I supposed to do?* We were not allowed to have, use, or look at mirrors because they represented vanity. I turned my back to the mirror and didn't dare look that way and see myself. My mind raced between the unlocked door and the forbidden mirror. My eyes were split between watching the door and getting my many clothes unzipped, unbuttoned, and off.

Once in the tub with water raining down, my ears strained to hear the words and sounds outside the door. This put me under extreme pressure. I finished my bath in a few minutes and turned the water off. I dried myself and hurried into my many long clothes while still in the tub and behind the shower curtain. Opening the curtain to step out, I discovered the floor had flooded. *What did I do wrong? What am I to do now?*

My heart beat faster than the rhythm of my racing thoughts and questions. What was I going to tell my unfamiliar grandma? I was afraid to put her good towel on the floor to help soak up the water. It might soil the towel, and she wouldn't like that. Did I wreck her floor? I felt terrible and took a moment to stand, catch my breath, and think of what I would say when I opened the door.

I walked out and told Grandma, "The floor got wet. I don't know why. I did what you said."

"Oh my child," Grandma said tip toeing into the bathroom and grabbing an old towel. "Look here! The shower curtain is on the outside of the tub. You must always put the shower curtain inside the bathtub when you take a shower. But you don't put it inside when you take a bath."

"I'm sorry, Grandma. I thought the curtain was to hide behind."

Grandma must have thought of me as really dumb, but

I was sure it would never happen again. I would not be so awestruck by all the new things that I would not see the small things. The curtain and tub area was about the size of the closet area we sponge bathed in, said prayers in, and changed clothes in while living in the colony. Afterward this all felt like an embarrassing big ordeal to me. If only I could have spiraled down the drain with the water and disappeared! Not knowing where to go or hide I went to the living room and sat with Mom as Grandma, wearing her strange shoes, click-clacked about between the kitchen and living room.

I watched Grandma spin a wheel on the strange, black, statue-type thing called a phone that stood on a stand in the hall. To me the phone looked like an image with big shoulders and a dress and with no head, arms, hands, legs, or feet. It had scared me earlier when it suddenly rang. It had a high pitch ring. It filled me with wonder, and I wanted to know how that bell rang when people called. I couldn't imagine how words could pass through a spiral wire and into a large bone-shaped piece in Grandma's hand and be heard. She just talked and seemed to be listening to someone.

Dad assumed we were in Indiana by now and called from the Veterans Hospital in Biloxi, Mississippi, where he remained a patient. Grandma talked with him. Then Mom spoke with Dad before putting the phone to Fred's ear. When he finished talking, he handed the receiver to me. I turned the phone the wrong way and needed help to get the receiver so I could hear Dad and he could hear me. This was my first time talking on a phone. Dad's voice sounded different. I didn't talk long. This was surely a strange experience. I felt sad for Dad locked up in that hospital.

"You live with your Grandma Long," he told each of us, "until I get out of this hospital."

Nobody knew when that would be — if ever. Dad sounded distraught. I felt like I was, and Mom looked like she was.

I found myself wondering what to do in this new environment and with all the foreign things that I had never experienced before. I didn't even know the names of a lot of the common items which I had never heard of. Perfume, deodorant, and toothpaste especially intrigued me. All we ever brushed our teeth with was a mixture of baking soda and salt.

What about all these strange people? According to our teaching, they were wicked heathens on their way to hell. I couldn't help but wonder if Mom would fit in with them since The Elder had condemned her to hell when she was in the colony? What could I do? I didn't want to go to hell, but how would I escape? I was frightened for my soul. I felt helpless and distressed inside even though I tried to never show a fraction of it. I prayed to my Lord for help and the strength to face each hour, each day, and my future.

Bedtime came and Grandma had three single beds all ready for Mom, Joan, and me in her largest bedroom. Fred's place to sleep was in the living room on a long, soft, green flowered seat thing called a couch or sofa. It seemed really nice for a bed. We were used to hard bench seats and simple homemade cotton mattresses.

"Good night!" Grandma said to everyone.

Another new expression for my vocabulary!

"Good night!" Mom said back to Grandma.

I wondered why she said good night. We never said those words.

Then I listened to the clicking as Grandma magically flipped switches turning out all the lights — unlike our kerosene lamps we had blown out every night. I knew when Grandma had climbed into her squeaky bed. Then everything became quiet.

I wasn't ready to go to sleep until I said my evening prayers. I had always knelt down in the closet with my head pointing north and my face toward the floor. I bowed with elbows, forearms and folded hands on the floor as I prayed. But here there was no closet to enter or door to shut and pray in secret like the Bible says in Matthew 6:6.

I hopped in bed, bowed to the north, pulled the sheet up over me as a curtain, and prayed my usual prayer. It was the original prayer The Elder had written for me at age nine: "I pray and give thanks to THEE LORD, for THY kindness to me in the name of JESUS. I pray for guidance that I may learn how I should behave before THEE, and that I may know to do those things that are pleasing in THY sight. Forgive me my trespasses as I forgive others, and allow me to see the way of THY righteousness, which can keep me from evil. For I desire some day to praise and honor THEE with an upright heart so I may be found worthy by THEE to receive a place within the bounds of THY kingdom. Amen"

With heart-felt sincerity I hoped God would hear me. I stretched out my exhausted body on the bed and laid my swollen face and my head full of thoughts on the pillow. Sleep wouldn't come to my overwhelmed mind or my aching eyes and body. Besides the walnut size knot stuck in my throat and the fist-size one that lay tightened in my stomach, a throbbing toothache still taunted my mouth. My mind raced in high gear into the night. I heard every sound inside and outside the house — every person's movement and strange noises. The refrigerator running, cars passing on the street haunted my mind. Shag's soft whines from the garage pierced my heart.

I really wanted to go to the garage and be with Shag, but I was scared to go there by myself. I wasn't afraid of the dark but of the worldly people in this giant city of about 38,000 people.

Then a shivering, unfamiliar sound startled me, nearly paralyzing my already tense body. I wondered if it was the sound of the seven trumpets and the end of the world. After trembling inside for awhile, nothing else happened. The last look at the clock let me know it was in the early morning when I knew others would be getting up shortly. Totally exhausted I finally dozed off.

Patricia Hochstetler

Chapter 2

Adjusting?

In the morning I asked, "What was that terrible sound last night?"

Grandma replied, "Oh, I never thought of telling you that trains run on a nearby track and blow their whistles in the morning before daylight. I'm used to the sound, and I don't notice it anymore."

I was still dumb-founded to hear voices when Grandma did something to the little wooden box on the counter. She saw my startled look.

"Oh, my Patricia, I forgot. You've never seen or heard anything like this before. It's called a radio."

"Is that what Uncle Carl had in his car? I didn't see a box though."

"Oh, I forgot about the one in the car. It's something like that one. It works the same way."

But how could people put their real voices inside the radio and it come out so we could hear them? Were their bodies invisible and in there too? I wanted to know. This added to my uncertainty about these worldly people. They occupied such tiny places. The Elder was right. These are heathen people doing strange things. I was troubled.

Soon we were all at the breakfast table. Still without an appetite I choked down a few bites of pancakes Mom made and decreed kosher. I wouldn't eat the eggs because I didn't know if the hens that laid them were caged. If not, the hens may have eaten something dead or unclean which defiled them and their eggs. My best excuse to Grandma when she urged us to eat was that I didn't feel well. I couldn't tell her about the chance of unclean eggs. Grandma wouldn't understand. I was also afraid to say anything about my toothache because she might insist I take her medicine for pain. She assumed I felt bad from the trip, and she was surely right about that.

Grandma left for work at Miles Laboratories where she had worked for many years putting caps on vitamin bottles. After she was gone I had a chance to ponder what was happening to me . . . to us.

It was hard to imagine how fast Mom, Fred, and Joan were changing. I thought they would have stayed more faithful to what we believed in the colony. Having left her box of clothes in Mississippi, Mom made some new worldly clothes for herself. With Joan forced to attend school she made worldly clothes for her too.

Fred's face and eye twitches lessened, and I was glad about that change. But he spent a lot of time riding a bicycle around the neighborhood. What about mingling in the wicked world? What about keeping the Sabbath holy and eating dietary food? Gelatin was forbidden by The Elder and Grandma made it in bright colors and some of them ate it.

Their facial expressions – frowns and smiles - began to reveal their emotions, and their actions changed almost daily. Did Mom care any more if she was doomed? And what about my brother and sister? Will their changes doom them to hell?

In Indiana most things were different from the colony including the trees, grasses, birds, houses, and especially the people. I was grateful for at least a few familiar sights I noticed here and there in Indiana like God's sky, sunrises, sunsets, clouds, rainbows, the moon and stars. The sun climbed to about the same height in the sky and rose and set at the same speed, but to me it seemed to travel much slower across the sky during these long days without much physical work. Yet I knew that by the clock, time was the same. I just wasn't working as hard and noticed time more. With less work I had time to wonder, to think, to reflect.

Each day was a challenge, but I looked for the familiar. The sunrises had the same beautiful, fresh start each day.

Adjusting?

Feather and pony tail clouds swished and swirled in the sky. Bright colors circled around the big orange fireball as it began to light up the world. Often a few welcoming, fluffy clouds waved around in the morning sky before dispersing. My evening activities were very different now. But the sunsets looked much the same as changing pastel colors outlined the disappearing sun accompanied by more feathery clouds. Sun rays poured down like strings of fog. Sometimes a bright *nava sonn*, (near sun) appeared. We later learned the worldly people called this a sun dog. There were bright, rainbow-colored spots on each side of the sun as it set. The illuminating reddish orange sun looked much the same and went down with the same speed, but the rolling Indiana landscape and many buildings made the sun appear to do more of a juggling act as it set behind the horizon. In the Mississippi Delta flat land the sun looked flat as if it rolled behind the horizon like water runs off a table and disappears.

My personal world was drastically different, but thankfully nature remained much the same. Black, white, or gray clouds still drifted in all shapes and sizes and looked much the same floating along in the same shades of crystal blue sky. Lightning and thunder looked and sounded much the same in the summer and fall. Indiana was not as hot. The moon appeared much the same. The stars were just as shiny, beautiful, and hard to count as ever.

The trees were quite different in Indiana and seemed more delicate. Indiana grass felt finer and appeared to be a darker green. The lawns were more cared for.

I missed the mocking birds we had in Mississippi. Birds in Indiana were different. Robins hopped around stretching poor worms until they snapped out of the ground, and then they ate them. We watched and were astonished at this sight.

Even the houses in Indiana were different, much bigger and more decorated. Barns here were huge and fancier than our Mississippi houses.

But it was the people that concerned me the most. These heathens were much louder, bolder, and talked a lot more. They expressed all kinds of emotions, feelings, and many more thoughts than the colony people did. The way they dressed was outrageously different in the amount of clothes, colors, and styles. They seemed to be more rushed but did less work. They moved at a jerkier pace and loafed around more and acted lazier. The colony people had a smoother pace and worked harder, and we got more done there with less commotion.

What the people in Indiana drank was a mystery to me. We were used to very hard, iron water, dry or canned milk, and no fruit juices or fancy drinks of any kind. Here the people drank weird, fizzy drinks they called 'pop.' They also had a black, bitter drink called coffee. I couldn't understand how anyone could drink that tar-looking water. But the weird, beer stuff Uncle Carl drank was absolutely outrageous. It made him really stink, and the cans smelled like rotten pears. I couldn't imagine how he could drink it. What it did to him was mind boggling and scary to see. Mom and Grandma said this drink was bad, and I didn't want to try it after what I had seen. I knew this drink had to be of the devil or have some kind of evil attached to it.

However I did meet some people who truly seemed sensible. They impressed me. As nice as they were, I couldn't see how they could be horrible heathens like I was taught. I began to wonder if there were good people in this new world who would really go to heaven. My tooth aches were getting so intense that I couldn't think about this anymore.

That next evening I experienced another shock, worse than the radio. Grandma turned on what she called a television. For the first time I saw tiny people moving around and staring at us while they talked.

As I watched television for the first time, many thoughts raced through my mind. *Surely people can't get into a box like that. Are they all midgets? How can they get in there and talk to us and look at us like that? Grandma said it was live television! It must be live because Uncle Carl talks back to them and argues with them.*

"Grandma," I asked, "can these people see us and hear what we say?"

She smiled but was careful not to embarrass me. "No, that's not the way it works"

It was impossible for me to comprehend that people could appear inside a box like this. Later when everyone left the living room and the television was still on, I went over to the television and looked behind it to find out how these people were reduced and got inside. I wasn't totally satisfied by Grandma's comment that they couldn't see or hear me, so I didn't go into the living room much for a while

I certainly hoped Grandma was right and the television people couldn't see us or ask me any questions. I had plenty of my own that needed answers. This concerned me until sometime later Mom convinced me that television people couldn't see us or ask me any questions. What a relief!

I felt overwhelmed just hearing and seeing the *common* things around me. I knew it would take time to understand the facts about these strange things. *Why did we have to leave the colony? Maybe The Elder was right. It was certainly simpler living in Lael Colony.*

On most days Uncle Carl had the television on from the moment he awoke until he went to bed at night. I couldn't understand what the people inside that big, square, strange-looking box were saying any better than the voices on the radio. I only occasionally understood some of their words. It sounded like mumble jumble to me, and I never really knew what was being discussed. I saw *unglaublich* (unbelievable) hoopla—people singing and dancing to what they called "music with a beat." *What's a beat?* I wondered.

Now I knew what singing people looked like. This dancing thing looked like wild horseplay, like young horses romping around in the pasture. It was inconceivable to me that people could throw their bodies around like they did. I saw no point in the singing or dancing. I had read about people in the Bible dancing and always wondered what it was. Now that I had seen it on television, I was surprised.

On top of everything else, each Sunday morning Grandma invited me to her church. Every Sunday I declined.

"Will you please come with me at least once?" Grandma

begged.

"I can't go," was always my answer, and she always looked disappointed.

Grandma kept trying to persuade me to go and didn't understand my plight and convicted feelings. Her hurt look bothered me, but I had to do what I was taught and could live with. She had no idea how far out of balance going to church would have thrown my already distorted life. According to The Elder's teachings all worldly churches were houses of Satan and his playground. I believed him. He gave us many warnings of the false prophets, teachers, and preachers in these worldly churches. I would have felt condemned even looking inside one and too guilty to be forgiven if I entered one.

These church places had *zirete* (ornament) glass windows with evil red colors, flowers, and people pictures. A sharp-pointed steeple aiming up to the sky stood atop them. Some churches had cross symbols on them, and others even had huge bells on top. *Why did they need those bells? Didn't people have clocks and watches?* Grandma often watched preachers on television and tried to get us to watch them too. I couldn't. My conscience would have bothered me too much. I felt torn between Grandma and my conscience. I just wanted to be back in the colony and away from all this.

From Uncle Carl talking about what was on television, I knew there were wars and rumors of wars going on. Many people were getting killed in Vietnam. On the streets of Elkhart and throughout the country, people were hurt and dying from automobile accidents. I thought it wasn't only destructive to their bodies. What about their souls? It sounded to me like the Hitler days were returning. This was scary!

The Elder had warned us for many years about killings and hard times coming. He often spoke of *The Black Book* written about the Nazi crimes against the Jewish people. It was published in 1946. I saw the book many times, but I was never allowed to read it. "Even though it's a Jewish book, it's still too bad for children to see or read," The Elder warned.

Now that I was living in Indiana, was this a part of the

hard times The Elder had predicted? Should I believe this television stuff? Should I allow it to enter my ears, my eyes, and my mind?

Mom discouraged us from watching the sinful television, so the only places for me were in the kitchen, in the bedroom, or in the garage with Shag. This world of bad amusement surrounded me. It felt so inconceivable I could barely hold it all in my head. What would be next?

Many times Uncle Carl called me a Dutchman and corrected my speech. "When are you going to learn to talk right?" he often asked. When he left the house, I felt more freedom and came out of the bedroom.

People had a hard time understanding me and frequently asked me to repeat myself. This added to my embarrassment. One time when I left the house a lady asked me, "Where are you from? Your accent doesn't sound like you are from the East or from the South."

I couldn't explain. I didn't know what they meant by accent. I wanted to hide and quit talking completely. If I lost my voice, people wouldn't expect me to talk. It felt like a bad dream that should have never come true. But it did. I faced it everyday without escape.

More relatives and people came to visit us and greeted us with a friendly, "Hi." I felt uncomfortable with every visitor for I was unable to use their worldly greeting. I was quickly embarrassed. I felt my face turn a painful, blood red. Even my ears felt like fire with each blush that rushed over my face every time strangers used the worldly "Hi" to speak to me. I wondered what was wrong with me and why I reacted this way. It felt bad, but I couldn't stop the blushing. When people came, they wanted to see all of us. Grandma or Mom called me out of the bedroom where I retreated once the work – like dishes and house cleaning – was done. Often during the day I went to the garage to be with Shag, wiped away his tears, and talked to him for comfort.

"Sometimes I wish I could cry like you do Shag," I confessed. "But I can't. It's wrong for me."

I read my Bible in both the garage and bedroom. I studied

the Bible verses, chapters, and all the headings of each chapter called scripture lines that I had memorized. Studying gave me a good reason to hide, and I was devoting my time to God's Word. I wanted to hide completely and forever.

Hours turned into days, and sometimes a few days felt like weeks. I lived in bondage to my fear of people, blushing, the food, our future, and what God thought of our leaving the colony. My teeth ached, and I wondered how on this earth I could escape all of this – fast!

I remember the first time in my life that I wrote a letter. It was written to my seven aunts, four uncles, and Grandpa back in the colony. I was unsure if they would respond. I wanted to know if they thought I had any chance of getting to heaven while living in this outside, wicked world. I also asked about them. I wanted to know about our animals, the birds, and The Elder, who had disappeared from the colony before we left. I sent the letter to the plantation manager hoping he would give it to Grandpa Miller. Then I patiently waited for an answer and struggled to cope.

After some adjusting of his own, Fred was the first to find a job and get out of the house. At 17 Fred went to work at Checkley's Drive-In, a nearby restaurant he could walk to. August came and Joan, my 15 year old sister, was forced by law to attend Concord School. After their 16th birthday children weren't forced to go to school. I was very thankful I turned 16 the day we left Mississippi. Although I had a great desire to learn, I didn't feel I could go to the public schools because of my shyness and painful toothaches.

I had plenty of time to think of what I wanted to do. According to Uncle Carl my speech was terrible. Since I didn't easily understand what worldly people said either, I decided to learn by studying the dictionary. I borrowed Grandma's copy of Webster's dictionary and started with the first letter. This kept me busy. I learned a lot while comforting Shag. Because it was cold in the garage, I tied a head-scarf over my mouth and cheeks and knotted it behind my head so my toothaches wouldn't become more severe and the swelling get worse.

Adjusting?

One day — based on comments by Grandma and others — Mom felt pressured to do something about my swollen face. "Patricia, when I find a job and have some money, I'll take you to a dentist," Mom announced. "He'll look at your teeth to see what can be done."

I was terrified! This was going too far. We weren't allowed to see doctors. They were of the world and it was wrong to see one if you trusted in God.

"Mom, you taught me that seeing a doctor is not right," I said seriously.

Was Mom really turning to the ways of the world? I knew she'd been condemned to hell by The Elder. Was she really starting on her way there by taking me to a doctor and heading down that broad, easy way that leads to destruction? Why would she want to take me to a doctor now? After all, I have been suffering with toothaches since I was four. By this time I felt well trained to endure the pain. Why couldn't I just be left alone as before? I had too much troubling my soul to deal with another stressful load of sin. Besides, I couldn't see any relief for my pain in it.

Mom tried to explain to me that a dentist might be okay. That's contrary to what she had taught me before, and I saw this as a choice between God's Way or the devil's way. I knew that I'd feel too guilty if I did something against God.

Mom reminded me, "You are a child under my care. If I choose to take you, the Bible says you are responsible to obey me. I would be accountable for my decision to take you to a doctor. Grandma is putting pressure on me to do something about why your face is swollen most of the time."

If it was wrong, she would be the one punished by God—not me. That helped, but not much.

I knew she was right about the responsibility part, but I feared for her. We stopped talking about this, and I had a few days to ponder the issue. I had been taught that seeing a doctor was wrong, and it bothered me that she wanted to do it. I decided not to say much more to Mom because she had enough to deal with. She was excommunicated from the colony, Dad was in the mental hospital, she was living

31

with her mother-in-law, and now she was under more pressure because of me. I didn't want to cause more hurt for her. I didn't want to disappoint her. I decided right then that as soon as I could, I would go back to the colony to be with God's people—even if I had to live alone in the woods and bayous of the Mississippi Delta.

The Lord was my shepherd, and He would provide for me. He helped me through many difficult things before. He spared my life, and I would not forsake Him now. Maybe this was a test of my faith in God. Then why didn't the knots in my throat and stomach go away? They were better, but not gone. Well, if I obeyed Mom, I'd be doing what I should and pleasing God according to *Ephesians 6:1*. If Mom is wrong by making me go to a doctor, she made it clear God would write it in her heavenly record and punish her, not me. Why would she want that? Well, I couldn't stop her. If she had my teeth fixed, maybe I wouldn't have the terrible toothaches anymore. Maybe I could think easier and learn more about the Bible so when I go back in the colony I would feel good and even work harder.

That was my decision, and the next time Mom said something to me about seeing a dentist I didn't resist. But I was still very concerned about her spirituality.

We now had lived in Indiana almost three months. Mom found a job at the restaurant where Fred worked. Joan went to school all day. I was left alone everyday with my alcoholic Uncle Carl. I certainly didn't like this arrangement. I spent much of my time in the garage with Shag. Lonely, he howled and cried almost every night. Each morning I cleaned the dried matter from his eyes. I had heard him howl and I tried to make him happy. He really needed me, and I needed him. He had reluctantly learned to be tied up with a chain. But he didn't adapt to this foreign world any better than I did. He looked as sad as I felt, and he seemed worse with each passing day.

One afternoon I told Shag, "It's okay for dogs to.whine and cry. You can cry all the tears you want on my long dress that people stare at and make fun of. I know you like my dress, and so do I. Shag, I feel like crying too. I need to go into the house to use the bathroom. I'll be back soon."

A few minutes later I returned to the garage. "Hey Shag, I'm back." He was sniffing and wagging his tail. His ears were alert, his brown eyes danced, and with every move he yapped. "Guess what! Mom's popping corn, and I ate a handful. Smell it? I know you like popcorn so I'll go back in the house and get us both some."

I made another trip to the house and Shag was waiting excitedly for me when I returned with our bowl of popcorn. "Let's see if you can still catch each kernel as good as you did in the colony. Snap! Crackle! Crunch! Yes, perfect! You caught it. Well, we practiced this for seven years. You're such a good dog, Shag," I sat down and wrapped my arms around his neck.

I didn't feel hungry for popcorn anyway. I enjoyed feeding Shag and gave him almost all the first bowl, one kernel at a time. I also gave him half my sandwich from lunch.

"Shag, I've never before told you how much you mean to me. We waited five long years after the tragic death of Teddy before you came giving us incredible joy. We didn't know if we would ever have another dog. You were the puppy blessing of a lifetime. It seemed God sent you to stay. Now here we are all cooped up in this garage in Indiana. It's too bad we both can't go back to Mississippi."

It was awfully hard to adjust, especially since I didn't want to!

Patricia Hochstetler

Chapter 3

The Dentist!

After Mom worked a few weeks, she made an appointment for me to see Dr. Stamp, Uncle Carl's dentist. Uncle Carl warned us, "This dentist is the most experienced, rough, tough and least expensive dentist in town."

While driving Mom and me to the dentist, Uncle Carl flooded us with all kinds of tales about his dentist. We were a few minutes early so we sat down in the reception area. Soon we were ushered into a small room with dental equipment everywhere. His nurse positioned me in the long, narrow, brown dentist chair to wait. Dr. Stamp, a short stocky, hunched over, elderly man hurriedly entered the room. He seemed to be looking at the floor constantly as he spoke. Then after his first look in my mouth, he said, "All of her teeth must be pulled. Before I can do anything she must go on an antibiotic pill for ten days to get rid of this serious infection. Then I can pull her teeth and make her dentures."

"Do you mean you can't save any of her teeth?" Mom asked.

"There are only four bottom front ones that aren't decayed, and they wouldn't hold any bridge work. I'm afraid her teeth can't be saved. Her teeth are soft, have deep crevasses, and are badly decayed and infected."

Mom had a distressed look but didn't say much.

Some years later Mom told me, "I felt terrible and thought it couldn't be that you would lose all your teeth, but I had to face the cruel reality."

I reviewed what I had experienced. Not only did I go to a doctor, the doctor was a man. Men weren't to touch women

35

under any condition. Then Mom said I would have to take the medicine the dentist prescribed. I had never taken any kind of pill or medicine before. It was forbidden. How would I be able to do all this against my religion? The sins were fast piling up in layers. I would have all my teeth pulled at age sixteen. How much closer to hell and the devil could I get? Doctors, medicine, this world, heathens, and now no teeth!

Mom made an appointment for me to actually have my teeth pulled ten days later. I felt helpless and hopeless. I was scared and didn't know what to expect. I questioned if this was really okay, but I had to obey. I resigned myself to the inevitable, and I did as Mom told me.

My thoughts went to the future when I would be back in the colony. I remembered Grandpa Miller had dentures before he went into the colony, and The Elder accepted him and I thought God accepted him too. Maybe I would be accepted. There were some positive things to consider. If my teeth were fixed I wouldn't need to hold my hand over my mouth any more. People wouldn't stare at my black front teeth with big holes in them. I wouldn't be concerned about cold air getting into my mouth and onto my face. There would be no more cavities and puss bags hanging in my mouth and around my teeth, and no more painful toothaches!

Ten days passed and I returned to have all my teeth pulled.

Mom tried to encourage me, "It won't hurt as bad as all the toothaches you've had in the past."

I wanted to believe her. How could it be any worse? That relieved the thought of physical stress and pain, but what about the mental torture of going to a doctor? I still felt guilty for going, yet went anyway. Dr. Stamp looked in my mouth, shook his head, and shared more bad news, "I can't pull her teeth today. There's still too much infection. I'll give you another prescription for ten more days. Make an appointment to come back, and I'll pull her teeth then."

Mom made the appointment to return in ten days.

After that ten days passed, the infection had cleared up and I even felt better physically. After his examination that day, Dr. Stamp chose to only take a third of my teeth out. They were all on the left side — top and bottom — up to the eye teeth. One bottom molar had decayed into the jawbone and even part of the jawbone was missing. He had to dig after small pieces of the roots.

The shots were not much worse than a big Mississippi mosquito bite. He started pulling teeth as soon as he was done giving me the shots and before my mouth was completely numb. I never said a word the entire time.

He asked Mom, "Is she always this quiet and still?"

"She's always quiet," Mom responded.

What Dr. Stamp didn't know was that he could have sawed off my arm, and I would have been just as quiet until I passed out. I really didn't believe any amount of pain or sadness would make me cry or scream. I wished this would have been only a dream that would fade away in time. Instead I faced a reality that would last all my life—no teeth, guilt, stress, and all the hidden emotions that went with it. The pain of right or wrong was far worse and outweighed any physical pain. I closed my eyes for a moment and tried to imagine this was someone else and not me sitting in that big chair under hot, bright lights with all kinds of shinny, silver tools dashing and flashing in and out of her mouth. Teeth kept exiting my mouth and stacking up in a pile on the tray.

A man, a big face, and his oversized hands were digging in my mouth. This didn't feel right, yet Mom was standing there watching. I was not to touch any man . . . not even my brother . . . if I could prevent it, but look what was happening. All the thoughts that flashed in my mind were torture— seeing a doctor, touching a man, no teeth—it was all wrong. I was extremely self-conscious and embarrassed at the way this dentist looked at me, knowing I looked different and "had such terrible teeth for a teenager" as he put it. This was about all I could tolerate in one day.

My heart pounded like a hammer striking a nail. I could feel rushes of blood coming up my neck and into my face each time he said something to me. At least the blood had a way out through each hole the doctor made when he pulled a tooth.

Dr. Stamp kept saying, "Spit. Spit."

He put white rag-looking stuff called gauze into my mouth. He pulled it out all red and bloody. How was I going to survive this ordeal. Maybe I would just bleed to death and there wouldn't be anything to worry about anymore. Mom was right. This pain was quick and mild compared to the severe toothache pain I had in the past, yet I felt worse with all these added emotional pressures. They made my pain unnatural.

Dr. Stamp asked, "Do you see that pile of teeth there? That's what the big three foot high rock out in the front of this office is made of. Those teeth are all cemented together, and your teeth will help make it even larger.

With all my teeth he could make at least one big stone, I thought.

"There's still some infection in your jaws, and I want to prevent any more. Now I want you on another antibiotic for seven more days," Dr. Stamp ordered. "Make another appointment a week from today, and I'll pull all the teeth on the right side."

Before we left his office he asked us, "Do you see how big and muscular my right hand is? It's from pulling hundreds of teeth for so many years."

As I walked out of the room with a lopsided mouth, the reality soaked in and struck hard. Mom scheduled another appointment in seven days and paid the nurse for my extractions. I went to the dentist's front yard to examine his tooth rock. It was real! Thousands of white teeth of every shape speckled all over the huge grayish rock. I silently went to the car light-headed and extremely speechless. I wondered how many teeth he had pulled and how many different mouths his hand had entered.

As Uncle Carl chauffeured us home, he said, "You're finally getting your teeth fixed. When will you stop wearing that gray, floor-dragging, bag of a dress you're wearing? If you get a job, they could hire you sweep and mop floors by just walking around with that dress on."

Not knowing what to say, I looked at Mom and she had a blank look on her face. When we arrived at Grandma's, I went to the bedroom and never left for the rest of the day, not even to eat.

The next day my mouth was terribly sore. I learned to sip through a straw, a new experience for me. I sat in the garage with Shag most of the day. He never complained as he sniffed and noticed my horrible stale-smelling, bloody breath and mouth. He whined and laid his head in my lap as I stroked his beautiful black head, ears, and the white mark running between his eyes. Suddenly silent tears dropped on Shag's head. He rolled his shiny, brown eyes up at me and whined. He didn't care if I cried.

I told Shag, "I don't care either, and if you're going to cry sometimes, I will too."

Then I felt guilty for my few tears.

Seven days later I returned to Dr. Stamp's office and sat in that same brown dental chair. While he worked, I stared at his high ceiling to keep from seeing his huge hands, especially his right one.

It felt harder to force myself to go each trip. It was hard to take knowing it was a repeat of what I had already been through. Now he pulled all my teeth on the right side — top and bottom — just as he had on the left side. I knew that after a week of healing I'd be in the dentist's office again to have all my front top and bottom teeth pulled.

The thought of going for the final pulling sounded good because it would be for the last time, but I still dreaded this visit even worse than the others. Dr. Stamp gave me more shots, and before I was completely numb he started to work. When he yanked on the first eyetooth, it felt like he was pulling my eye out! Now that was tough to take, but I never said a word or flinched.

Dr. Stamp hurriedly snapped out each tooth, and he explained, "Your front teeth have such shallow roots. It's like picking corn off of a cob, especially these four good bottom ones." When he finished he told Mom, "Now make an appointment to return in three weeks. This will allow enough time to heal up, and I want her on an antibiotic for ten more days. If the infection and swelling are gone, we'll make impressions and put the dentures in a week later."

Walking out of the dentist's office without a tooth in my mouth was the worst feeling yet. Reality invaded my entire head, mind, and mouth. It seemed both a blessing that the pulling was over and a curse that all my teeth were gone. My mouth collapsed. I had to make a conscious effort to drop my chin or it felt like it would touch the end of my nose. My mouth was like an empty cave. I eased into the car with my head down and mouth covered. I would only shake my head to answer questions. Once at Grandma's house I once again went straight to the bedroom.

Uncle Carl had teased and given me a rough time many prior days when he was drinking. This day he was a little more gentle when he said, "If you don't eat more, you'll blow away when you go outside."

In the colony I always wanted to put weight on my barely five feet tall frame, but I never could. I never weighed more than 99 pounds. Now I was well below that and could only drink liquids.

Before the second day passed Uncle Carl was laughing and calling, "Now bring your skeleton to the table, and try to put some meat on those bones." I was Uncle Carl's prime joke and picking target. He picked on me like I was the weakest chicken in our chicken coop back at the colony.

"Hey, you toothless old Dutchman granny – when are you going to start talking plain English?" he would bellow.

"I don't know," I replied, hung my head, and covered my mouth with my hand.

Then many unfamiliar curse words rolled off his stiff tongue, appalling phrases fell from his shaky lips, as ridiculous remarks staggered out of his slobbering mouth.

I stayed in the garage and only went into the house to use the bathroom, or if Uncle Carl had left the house – which was seldom and that was usually to get alcohol or cigarettes. He would be back too soon and pass out on the couch with a cigarette burning in his ashtray on the floor.

Many times his dirty, ashy and sometimes burning cigarette butts fell on Grandma's wonderful carpet leaving black, hard, tar-looking burnt spots. Often when I came into the house and smelled his cigarettes, I put them out while he was snoring on the couch. Uncle Carl's disrespect for other people, what he did to Grandma's house, and the way he talked to her and treated her was terrible. This was stressful for me to see, but I guess she was used to him.

I will never become accustomed to that kind of life.

Returning to Lael Colony was my goal – now stronger than ever.

Patricia Hochstetler

Chapter 4

Shag

I made sure to spend most of my days in the garage with Shag, my buddy. He taught me to cry, and it developed into a daily routine. Shag whined, laid his head tightly on my lap, and pressed down a bit while I stroked his head. My tears fell on him. Sometimes he put his front feet in my lap and lay against me. I felt guilty for crying, yet I felt relief.

Shag and I comforted each other. In fact if Shag noticed me crying, he would lick the tears off my hands. He would look at me and whimper as if it upset him that I cried. It seemed our roles had reversed, and he wanted to comfort me.

"I'd like to stop crying, Shag," I whispered. "I wish I could make it like it used to be, but I don't know how." I tried to cheer him up, but he still noticed and seemed concerned. He totally accepted me and my tears. We bonded even closer than we had in our previous seven years.

Then one day Mom overheard a neighbor talking to Grandma. "Bertha, that dog at your house is a nuisance!" she complained. "It's keeping us awake at night. You have to do something."

Grandma didn't like dogs anyway, so it wasn't long after that when she announced, "I can't sleep good with Shag whining at night. I must get my rest so I can go to work every morning." Nothing happened immediately.

I didn't mind if Shag kept me awake. I couldn't sleep very well anyway with everything so new and strange. I knew I had to comfort Shag. I thought he would adjust as we learned to live in this new world together.

It wasn't long before I heard Uncle Carl talking to Grandma, "For $10.00 I can take Shag to the vet and have him put to sleep."

She didn't say anything. But I suddenly had a lot to think about. *DEAD! That meant Shag would be gone forever. Not Shag! It wouldn't happen if I had anything to say about it! He is now my best friend.*

At one time I thought Fred was my best friend and work buddy, but since he found a job at the restaurant he seemed to abandon me. In the evening he took bike rides and visited with other boys in the neighborhood. He even started playing, of all things, with a fancy looking round thing with sewed stitches on it. They called it a ball. They threw and hit that ball lots of places with a long round club. I didn't understand their ball playing game at all. Fred didn't seem to think there was anything wrong with playing with that white ball.

Once I hid behind Grandma's shrubs and watched them play in the empty lot behind her house. Then someone saw me. I was gone like a streak of lightning and hid in a flash before the worldly boys could make fun of me and my clothes.

Fred didn't dress and look as different as I did. After Dad went to the hospital and before we left the Mississippi Delta, Fred drove tractor and talked to a few people outside our colony. He wasn't as shy as I was, and he was more prepared to face our new world. I missed talking to him.

Because she was 15, Joan had to go to Concord School all day, and in the evening she had homework. She had enough of her own problems adjusting to everything including the public school which was completely different from our Lael Parochial School. I felt sorry for her and was certainly glad I wasn't forced to go to the public school. She had to wear gym shorts and take showers with other girls. Some days when she had gym class she became sick when it was time to go to school, and she stayed home. She quit wearing her heavy, long, gray dress and matching gray head covering. She wore a thinner mid-calf length skirt, a blouse that Mom made, and no head covering. Even though I was curious and had an interest in her schoolwork and learning, it would have been extremely difficult for me to attend public school with my shyness and without teeth.

So who would I talk to during the day if my uncle succeeded with his cruel suggestion about Shag? I knew I couldn't talk to him about it. He didn't make much sense to me anyway. I didn't really think he would kill Shag, but what if he did?

What if this really did happen to Shag, my pal? I knew he always waited in the garage for me. When I needed a place to go or get out of the house, I went to be with Shag. If I wanted someone to talk to, or look eyeball to eyeball with, and cry with, or just sit beside without any words at all, Shag was there. I enjoyed putting my hands on his head and thinking as we would rest. Who would I physically have to touch and comfort and go to for comfort without Shag? Who would understand like he does? Who would always accept me just as I was, even with no teeth? Who would always have a friendly welcome every time I appeared? Who would always look at me with big, brown eyes and grin like he did, no matter how hard things were for him or me? This terrible thing Uncle Carl suggested couldn't happen!

When Shag was on the end of a chain, he barked at everything strange he saw — people, cars, and foreign objects. He jerked, pulled, and wouldn't accept it. Our Shag had never worn a collar before, been tied up with a chain, or locked up in a building. He always went free as a bird in the wind, roaming where ever he wished.

"Shag, there is something too terrible to talk to you about. But I have to. You know we didn't choose you. You chose us. As a tiny, lost, stray puppy with no place to go or call home, you came to live with us, and we accepted you and fed you. You were wandering down that old gravel road and turned into our drive and came to our house on your own, and we took you in. We accepted you and your brother, Shorty, into our family."

Shag was a good listener. There was so much I needed to say. My pain was almost more than I could bear. The fear of losing him added to my sense of uncertainty. His were the pair of ears I so desperately needed, but he could offer no words of wisdom or advice. He could only provide love. And he did!

"Shag, we fed you the best we could afford. You never went hungry unless we did. You never ate store bought dog food. You only ate table scraps and leftovers from our meals, and you appreciated them. That was the reason I didn't eat much at times, so there would be something left for you. If we had no food leftover, we cooked you a bowl of corn meal mush. You were always thankful. On rainy days when we couldn't work in the fields, I worked hard grinding corn for corn meal so we all had food, even you. I enjoyed turning the handle on that old hand grinder as long as I was in the barn with you by my side. We could watch the nesting pigeons together while I was grinding. I wish I had a corn grinder handle to turn now. Shag, you can cry all the tears you want on my dress. I'll catch them. Flood it! I don't care. But remember, Shag, you don't have a soul to be concerned about like people do — like I do"

That was my last private talk with Shag. I cried like I had never cried before. Whining, Shag acted like he really knew something was wrong. It was worse this time, but he didn't understand why. He only lay his chin on my lap and looked at me with his big, brown eyes, nudging my hands to move them. He licked tears from my checks as though he was again trying to comfort me instead of me comforting him.

With a knot in my throat I kept saying to him, "Shag, you just don't know what's about to happen. You don't know! You just don't know. I can't believe it. Why, why, oh, why you? Why can't it be me going instead of you? You could adjust to this world easier than I can. You're not so shy. You can face people. You don't blush every time someone looks at you or talks to you. They don't ask you why you turn so red. You have nice teeth and can eat well with them but not me. I know you could make it if they'd let you. I know you could. But I don't know if I can. It looks impossible to me. You're not afraid to speak out, but I can't. You bark when you can't take things or feel bad. You show your feelings when you hurt or when you're happy or sad. I can't! Shag, I've learned a lot from you — mostly how to cry and how to show emotions. But I can't do these things with people. We aren't to use the word love and I haven't before, but Shag, I love you. I don't want you to go and leave me all alone in this strange, big, bad world. No, it can't be."

The next day my uncle had the deadly appointment with Dr. Shaffer, a veterinarian. It was Saturday, our Sabbath, which I still observed. Fred stopped keeping it because of his job. He took off work this Saturday, and my uncle said he had to go along to Shag's appointment. Shag liked cooked corn meal mush, chicken bones, and leftovers from the dinner table. That's what he ate for his last meal. Mom cooked the corn meal especially for Shag, and he was beginning to eat better by now. He was very healthy. After I saw Shag enjoy his last meal, I said good-bye to him in the garage and went to the bedroom so I wouldn't have to see him leave.

I heard my uncle's car back out the drive. It was that same old, copper bullet that hauled Shag and all of us from Mississippi to Indiana. Now Shag was taking his death ride in it. I looked out the bedroom window for one last glance hoping to see Shag. That old car looked more like a hearse or worse, an oversized coffin on wheels.

Thoughts flew through my mind of how God could intervene and stop my uncle from doing this terrible thing. I felt helpless. I imagined them getting in a minor accident or having a flat tire and Shag would escape and find his way back to us at Grandma's house. It never happened. I had many dreams for years after that. I often dreamed Shag was only lost, that he found his way back to us, and we were extremely joyful and happy to see him again.

Now there was no reason to go to the garage. Shag wasn't there. It was dark, quiet, lonely, and full of cobwebs that I never noticed before. It only made me ask, "Why did Shag have to go? He was so good . . . such a nice dog . . . he never hurt anyone. He comforted me and made me feel needed. I only wanted to know why."

I wanted him back so badly and knew it could never be. At least I didn't have to go with my uncle when he took Shag to the veterinarian. He forced my poor brother to go instead.

Fred returned and couldn't talk. Later he told me all about his experience. With moist, brown eyes even 30 years later he said, "I was ordered to take Shag to the car and from the car into the veterinarian's office for them to kill him. They told me to put Shag on a table. Then I watched the doctor give him that lethal shot, and he lay down and died before my eyes. My friend! Our pet! Gone forever!. I didn't have a choice in the matter. It was just so hard to do.

"Our uncle told the veterinarian we would bury Shag, and he made me carry Shag's warm, lifeless body to the car. He drove to our Aunt Marie's house, picked a burial spot, and I had to dig Shag's grave and carry his limp body from the car to his grave and cover him up with dirt. All that really tore me up. It was like I knew Shag was dead, but he didn't know it and was still my friend. The hurt nearly killed me!"

For 12 years we had been taught not to kill anything except snakes. Grandma and Uncle Carl had forced Fred to watch while our friend of seven years was killed.

Shag wasn't wanted by some in and around Grandma's house, and we had no place to call home for Shag or us, or any money to board him. Shag wasn't given enough time to adjust. It ripped our family up knowing our childhood friend was gone forever.

We were forced to cope with his death. Now I really wanted to put on sackcloth and ashes to mourn Shag's unjust death. This was different from all the grasshoppers and bugs I tried to save that were sprayed with insecticide in the cotton fields. They died and we had pretend burials for them and forgot them. We couldn't forget Shag.

In the dark garage with Shag — that's where I felt most comfortable in Indiana. If I knew someone was coming, the garage was where I went as first choice, the bedroom as second choice. If I was in the house, there was more of a chance of someone seeing me. There was a possibility I would be called out of the bedroom and sized-up by strangers.

I had no reason to be in the garage now that Shag was gone. I gave the excuse that I wanted to study where it was quiet, but it didn't work. I couldn't concentrate. Shag was all I thought of. I felt like I was grasping for something to hang on to, to make sense of, and to make life worth living. If I couldn't find it, I wanted an amen to my life.

Patricia Hochstetler

Chapter 5

Rock Bottom

It was early morning and I felt like an egg that had fallen out of its nest in a storm and shattered prematurely.

I felt like a baby chick who had lost its opportunity to crack its shell, breathe the clean fresh air, stick its head out for a peek, and stand on its feet. My tears dripped like blood leaving both stains and scars. Weakness and fear filled my entire body from the soles of my feet to the ends of each hair on my head. I trembled and was sure this cruel, new world would kill me. I wanted back in my lost shell.

I was tired of my empty toothless mouth. I wanted my teeth! I wanted to hide, melt like ice cream on a hot summer day, quietly drift through society as an invisible mist, and then run down through the cracks and soak into the ground like water disappearing from the face of the earth.

My greatest desire was to be back in Lael Colony where I grew up with God's chosen Amish-Jewish people. But our past was history and could not be relived. It was impossible to change Mom's excommunication, Dad's hospitalization, our exit from the colony, our move to Indiana, and my lost teeth. There had to be a way for me to go back into the colony. Wasn't there a way to make my life worth living? If not, I wanted it all to end and the sooner the better.

Cars raced back and forth on the busy street outside the window. The sky was one mass of smooth, gloomy gray. On that cool fall Monday morning a stale, stuffy odor filled the air. Uncle Carl's cigarette smoke, which always made me ill, was mixed with the air from Grandma's Michigan style basement, an alcove of cement and dirt below the house.

Mom and everyone else had gone to work, school or somewhere else for the day. Grandma took Uncle Carl to spend the day at Aunt Marie's so he could recover from his all night drinking binge. Grandma insisted that he stay there. I knew nobody else would be in the house all day. I sat alone in the bedroom I shared with my mom and sister. I stared at the cold, tan and red-streaked linoleum floor. The living room clock ticking echoed in my ears. There were none of Shag's whines coming from the garage.

Hot tears silently trickled down my cold checks. There was no Shag to lick up the tears he had taught me to cry. Soon tears flowed from my eyes in streams falling in many directions. Unable to keep my composure I cried aloud for the first time in my life that I could remember. I thought, *I don't care. Nobody can hear me but God, and He knows how I feel anyway.* I began sobbing louder and louder. I wanted to quit, but for some reason I couldn't. I got up and began walking to the living room and then back to my bedroom crying.

There were bursts of extreme sobbing. Exhausted I would cry softly for awhile. I told myself, "You must control this crying." I would get my loud crying under control and lay down quietly with tears gushing like a faucet from my eyes. Then suddenly I would uncontrollably burst into a hard cry again and moan and groan. That was something else I had never done before.

I couldn't think of any reason why I acted like this. I paced the house from bedroom to living room and then on to the kitchen. Back and forth I went time after time. When I finished crying, moaning, and groaning out loud I felt so full of frustrations I wanted to scream. But that, too, was forbidden. I always wondered if I could, but never wanted to try because of the sin connected with it.

I had never been left alone before. Now I was, and the urge to scream was growing stronger and stronger! With tears flowing out of control I finally surrendered to my pain and screamed out loud for the first time that I could remember. I surprised myself. I could really scream. Then I continued to cry, moan, and groan. I screamed several times more and threw myself on the couch. When it became soaked with my tears, I got up and went to my bed and repeated the out cry. I was shocked to realize that I felt angry for the first time. I felt scared, angry, hurt, sick, and desperate. I wanted to know why all of this was happening to me.

Pacing from the living room to the kitchen, I screamed as loud as I could three times. Suddenly it dawned on me that the neighbors might hear me acting like this, get alarmed, and come over to see what was wrong. This shocked me back to my senses. I quieted down with only a few more low screams.

My throat hurt and felt swollen and was accompanied by the ever-present knot. A shadow of shame fell over me. What had I just done? Guilt filled every pore of my body. My mind struggled with the pressure. I wondered, *Did Jesus ever scream? I know He got angry in the temple. But did I have any good reason to scream and would He forgive me?* I immediately added screaming and anger to my growing list of known sins I had committed since I left the colony. I felt bad, evil, sinful, and my conscience gnawed at me viciously.

All my life I had tried very hard to be good, to do right, and to please God in everything. Now I felt trapped in a wicked world. I was forced to see a doctor, and I had allowed myself to scream and get angry. I thought, *Maybe I had done more evil not knowing it and would be condemned for it.* I knew Shag would have been hysterical if he heard and saw me that day. But what did God think of me at that moment?

I sobbed and allowed myself to feel angry anyhow. Was I angry because they killed my best friend, Shag? I missed him so terribly. Why? Why did he have to go? He didn't deserve it. Why did they do it to him? He was a good dog. He only cried and was loud in his howling, barking, and screaming like any normal dog in distress. I wondered if he ever felt angry at what was happening to him. His punishment was death.

Why can't mine be too? I've cried, screamed, and gotten angry. Now I have so many sinful marks in God's heavenly record. Maybe He will strike me dead for all of this sinning. I'm not answering for my sins by severe tooth pains anymore, only swollen sore gums, but the pain of living in this new world is a far worse punishment.

I don't have a home, a room to call my own, or my own bed. I feel like an orphan in a foreign land. I can't understand these people. The evil radio and television don't make sense to me. I can't listen to them to learn because I've been taught such things of the outside world are so extremely sinful. I'm too backward to speak with outside people. The more I thought of these things, desperate and lonely feeling would cause me to burst out crying. My sobs would eventually weaken to soft whimpers and *de moot lowse* (the low mood) would overwhelm me again.

I had to stop crying, but I simply couldn't. There was no way I would answer the door if anyone came. That lump in my throat now felt the size of a lemon that was still on a branch scratching and wearing my throat raw. I began to shake and quiver almost uncontrollably and gasp for air.

Suddenly I thought, *Will I lose my mind like Dad did and go to a hospital?* This scared me even more. The despair was worse at that moment than when I was ten and almost died. I was bad physically then, so ill I didn't care what happened to me and I drifted off into unconsciousness. But my emotions were fine. I wasn't at all scared either. I was simply too weak to care, respond, or hurt. Now, I hurt down to the marrow in every one of my bones and to the core of my heart.

Not only did my mouth hurt and stink like stale blood, my head ached and felt beaten and bruised by my own thoughts. My purple heart was broken and hurting so deeply I didn't know what to do for relief. My emotions had exploded out of control for the first time in my life, and I allowed them to. I was so much worse than I had ever felt in my entire life, and I wondered why I couldn't somehow change it or just lie down and die instantly like Shag did. I missed him so terribly. Why did he have to go? Why didn't my uncle have the veterinarian give me the shot instead?

If I were dead and all this pain was over, there would

be no more headaches, sore mouth, hurting eyes, knotted sore throat, or lumps of pain in my stomach. Heartache would be gone, emotions calm again, and no more questions of — why? It sounded so good, if only I could make it happen without doing anything drastic or wrong like suicide. I was taught if anyone did commit suicide, it was murder, and they were hell-bound for sure because the Bible says, "*Thou shalt not kill.*" I didn't want to go to hell and burn forever and ever, so suicide was out of the question even though I really wanted to die.

After my teeth were pulled I thought I looked like a really old, dead person. Why couldn't the dentist have just pulled my head off rather than only pulling all the teeth out of it? I wouldn't have suffered as much.

But I really didn't want to weight Mom down any more with my burdens. She was already hurting so badly. I knew I couldn't tell her how I felt.

At rock bottom I visualized, wished, and prayed that someone would approach me and ask, "Do you confess to believe in God, or do you have a Bible?" According to what The Elder had taught, they would kill me if I had said yes. That would have solved my problem.

I would have waited willingly for my end to come. Instant death would have been much easier — no torture, pain, suffering, guilt, or shame, only painless relief and relaxation. Then I could put to practice what I was taught to do. I would die for my faith.

When I came into this foreign world, I thought sure someone would ask me this question, but nobody ever did. I had been taught if someone hit me on one cheek, I was to turn the other. Much to my surprise nobody ever tried that either. It was drilled into me that these things would happen in this outside world of wickedness, and I was prepared for it. Yes, I truly believed it would. I was NOT prepared to live.

If only God would have returned at that moment, or allowed me to stop breathing, that would have been the greatest blessing on earth. I wished I were dust and the wind would gracefully lift me up and blow me away f-o-r-e-v-e-r.

If only it would keep me sailing straight to heaven where I truly wanted to be!

I hadn't stopped crying and it was afternoon already. Eventually I came back to my senses. Sitting in a living room chair I realized lunchtime had long passed. I didn't care, and I was not the least bit hungry. But I had to change something before Mom, Fred, and Grandma got home from work and Joan from school. I still couldn't make myself stop crying, and I didn't want anyone to know, hear, or see me. God knew how I felt. I wondered if there was anyone in the whole world that could hurt as bad as I did at that moment. I allowed myself to feel it, think it, say it, and know it. Should I have allowed myself to feel all this? That was my question. I began praying and talking to God out loud, the first time I ever heard my own voice in prayer. Women and children were to pray silently.

In Grandma's living room I said to God, "I know You love me and care about me even if nobody else in the whole, wide world does. You know I have never wanted anything more than to please You and do what is right. I will trust You totally for help. You know how helpless I feel right now. I have no teeth, I can't eat much, and I don't even want to. I have no work to do, I feel useless, and no-one needs me . . . nobody at all! I'm too shy to get out into this scary world with all these worldly people that I can't understand. They are all supposed to be evil heathens. I know so little about living or how to live in this foreign world. What should I do, Oh Lord? Please show me and help me. Amen"

By this time I had worn a path across Grandma's elegant tan living room carpet from the front door to the kitchen. I feared someone would see the carpet smashed down and the couch soaked with tears. I was afraid my clothes would show the river of tears that I had shed. Throughout the afternoon I lay down on the couch or bed and cried softly, and then when another big burst of tears came, I arose and paced the floor again.

After I let all of my feelings out, I continued sobbing in loneliness. Tears trickled down my checks. Finally I lay down on the couch in total exhaustion. I gazed out the picture window across the room and watched the trees swaying in the breeze while I prayed.

My body was jerking hard, and my throat knot had doubled in size. I didn't understand how I could live through this entire ordeal. I lay there with thoughts streaming through my head faster than the tears that had run down my face. I wondered if people could run out of tears, and soon I had no more tears left in me. I couldn't even think of anything that would make me cry now - not even Shag. *Why did my tears dry up now when earlier I had wanted so desperately to make them stop but couldn't?*

I didn't understand what I was feeling about myself. I was emotionally numb. I couldn't keep my body from jerking. Since this had never happened to me before, I wondered if something had gone wrong with me and if I would stay this way. I prayed for Christ to return before Mom came home. Once again, that seemed to be my only way out. With dry eyes I stared at the white ceiling. Exhausted, I wished I could go to sleep and never wake up.

I did awaken about two hours later just minutes before Mom came home. I wasn't jerking and didn't cry, but my eyes burned and felt puffy and strange. I went to the bathroom and that forbidden mirror reflected the truth. I looked like a different person. My eyes were swollen and red. I washed my face with cold water in hopes that would refresh me and the swelling would go away. Could crying cause the swelling, or was something really wrong with me?

I went to my bedroom and lay on my bed fearful that someone would come and find me. It was as though water had flowed through me like a broken dam and washed me out from within. I felt like a balloon that had burst and was left totally deflated, flat, void of everything good and bad. I didn't want to think or move.

I didn't want Mom to ask any questions about what had happened or if something was wrong. Above all else I didn't want her to worry any more because of the load she already had. My greatest fear was that someone would discover the way that I spent the entire day. Heaven forbid!

Minutes before everyone was scheduled to get home I decided to go to bed and claim I felt sick, which I really did. Every thread of flesh between my head and toes hurt.

I didn't feel good enough to get up or eat. I lay in bed and faced the wall all evening and remained as quiet as my thoughts. I listened to Mom, Grandma, my brother, sister and uncle talk while they ate. The day blended with the night. I never saw the sun set. Darkness fell and so did my spirit.

The evening passed and finally everyone went to bed. I lay wide-awake most of the night. At 1 a.m., after I knew everyone was asleep, I got up and went to the bathroom and checked to see if my eyes looked any better. They didn't. My only hope was to try to sleep and still plan to say I didn't feel well in the morning. I finally dozed off for a few minutes. When waking I wondered once more if anyone suspected anything. I didn't want this to ever happen again. It shamed me to think I had been so out of control.

Could it get worse? Would it ever get better?

Chapter 6

Is Return Possible?

Morning came and I didn't get up until everyone left the house except my drunken uncle. I heard him come home from a drinking binge at 3 a.m. and I knew he would sleep late.

I quietly got up and tried to get some liquids down. This morning I had no tears or urge for any. I prayed a lot which felt good, and I was in the right frame of mind to think rationally. I had to come to grips with myself and decided what I wanted to do and how to do it. I had these options: go crazy, feel sorry for myself, cry my life away, try to find someone for a crutch to hold me up, help myself the best I could, or ask God for more help.

I asked God for more help!

For awhile I felt a deep, calm peace inside almost as deep as my hurt was the day before. I went to the bathroom and stared into that non-lying mirror. My eyes looked a little better, but they were far from normal. I wondered why I cried so uncontrollably the day before. Why did I feel the weight of the world crash in on me? Why wouldn't this nightmare and its reoccurring flashes go away?

I went to my bedroom and for a few minutes I laid on the bed with my wounded will. I was listless, helpless, hopeless and any other 'less' that could be experienced. I felt numb and emotionless most of the day and tried to think of what I could do to feel better and what changes I could make about myself. I knew I was out of sync with my new world.

I rehearsed the Bible chapter headings that I had learned in the colony and all the nine blocks of scripture that The

Elder had given us to learn. I kept thinking and repeating the Bible verse I learned years ago. *Oh that I had wings like a dove! For then would I fly away, and be at rest.* This verse kept playing in my head over and over again. I wanted a way out of it all. I wanted a place of peace where there would be no more hurting.

I knew I couldn't fly even though I had many dreams of doing so, but maybe I could be at rest somehow, somewhere, someday. Writing all this now feels like that throat knot has returned. That verse from Psalms allowed me to fantasize about what it would be like to be free from all the pressures that I felt. I never wanted to talk about all of this or look back on it. I felt like a total misfit.

For days my mind wondered from place to place as I tried to think how I could get back to the colony. If I planned to get there, I needed some money. I would need a job so I could buy a bus ticket. I could leave as soon as I got my dentures. I needed to keep studying God's Word so I'd still know as much as I did when I left and perhaps even more. Maybe I would be accepted in the colony if I was not with my family.

I especially liked Psalms and Proverbs. Reading chapter after chapter from them gave me courage. One day I decided to find the verse that had stuck in my mind all this time, Psalm 55:6, and I read the entire chapter. Much to my surprise I felt more verses in that chapter fit me. Then I clung to verse 16 and rehearsed them together.

These verses brought reassurance as the sound of my voice echoed in the room as I would quote, *Oh, that I had wings like a dove! For then would I fly away, and be at rest.* Then in quiet reverence I would add, *As for me, I will call upon God, and the Lord shall save me.* For weeks this chapter provided me with inner strength as I struggled to get a grip on life again. I was no longer afraid to cry. After all Jesus wept, so weeping or crying couldn't possibly be evil. But I still didn't want anyone to see me cry.

I had a burning desire to learn more that would help me understand the people I was going to be around until I returned to the colony. I studied the dictionary and found it most interesting. I discovered I didn't have to have my teeth to memorize well. I still had my brain.

When Mom saw me and approached, I would comment, "I'm going to learn it all."

She would encourage me, "That's good. Learn all you can."

"I want to understand these people around here."

I worked hard at writing down the many words people used that I didn't know. I found out that even the dictionary didn't have some of the words they used. They called it slang. There were some words they called 'fad' words. Those were hard to deal with too. Then there were some words that were worse.

I couldn't wait until my mouth was healed. I would have some teeth even if they were false ones. Then maybe I could eat, talk, and think about letting someone see me. Maybe I could even learn to smile now that I was trying all those new things like crying, doctors, medicine, strange foods, and praying out loud when alone. I was sure that when I got my new teeth and could see people again, I would still be unable to keep from blushing and getting that red-hot feeling all the time when they looked at me or said, "Hi." I knew that if I was going to survive in this world of so many people, I had to overcome my shyness.

I set that as my first goal after I got my teeth.

Questions about my future flooded my mind and I realized that I needed more time.

Well, at least I had one goal to work toward before I got a job. My eyes felt and looked better now and I hoped I would never need to hide again. Just as I was getting up my nerve and self-confidence, Mom came home and remarked, "Your eyes look puffy."

"Oh Mom! Do you think the swelling is from my teeth being pulled and my sore mouth?" I asked.

"It's possible."

I thought Mom didn't understand the cause, and I didn't say much more.

"Don't worry, Mom. The swelling will soon be gone," I assured her and went to bed early.

I didn't want Mom to worry about me for she had enough pressure and disappointments of her own. She was also trying to learn a new job and work in the public again after all her years in isolation. The four of us living at Grandma's was costing her money and this bothered Mom. Each week Grandma would say, "Well, my grocery bill has more than tripled."

Mom encouraged us to only eat what we needed and no more. Unable to eat much without teeth, I drank liquids and tried to limit those too. Most of the food was strange to me, and I feared eating something that had touched lard or bacon.

I still felt like an orphan in this foreign land. I felt I should resist it and run from it if I wanted to get to heaven. Eating anything not kosher would make me unclean and evil. The world and food around me weren't going to change. When others turned on television and radios, I was forced to hear them against my will. This made me understand more, but I wouldn't intentionally sit and watch or listen to them. The television was twice as sinful as the radio because of both seeing and hearing it. I stayed in the bedroom most of the time studying. I didn't even want to come out to eat. Patiently I waited to heal, get my teeth, and go back to the colony. I learned to be content.

Still I desperately wanted to go back where I came from as soon as possible and to find out if I would be accepted there. I was even willing to live in the woods near a bayou. I pictured how I would have my own tent, cook my own food, and walk to the Sabbath meetings by myself. I would work in the fields beside my aunts, uncles, and Grandpa Miller even if I couldn't talk with them.

I imagined a very quiet world. It would allow me to be more spiritual, and I could learn more than one Bible verse a day. Learning was easy for me and I thought since The Elder had learned the entire Bible, I could too. My spirit rose and I began living on the fantasy of returning to the colony someday.

Much to my surprise and delight I received the first letter in my life while at Grandma's address. This was *unglaubich goot* (unbelievably good). My aunts, uncles, and Grandpa answered the letter I sent them. They told me they were all fine and what they were doing in the cotton fields. They wrote that they saw an animal control truck stop at our house but it soon left. The dogs we left behind would come and go from our empty house. They said my question concerning The Elder was not an easy one. They had received a small scripture study sheet from Oregon which they felt was possibly from him, but they weren't sure. They said they saw us leave that dark, dark night and were afraid the flashlight they blinked didn't give enough light to let us know of their farewells. They had hoped we could feel their concern.

I had asked if they thought I stood a chance of entering heaven if I lived in this outside world. At first it seemed they encouraged me to do my best, but they didn't feel one could be in the world and not be part of it. They said they were watching and waiting. They stated that patience works wonders and challenged me to follow the words of David, "Wait on THE LORD." They asked me not to be hurt if they didn't write anymore because of the separation The Elder had put between our families after Mom's excommunication. They said writing to me made them feel guilty.

I missed them so much! It was wonderful to hear from family in the colony this one time, even if I never would again. Their letter gave me no hope of heaven unless I could get back into the colony. As I now saw it, that sounded hopeless. All I could do was wait until I found a way back there and then try again. I was definitely willing to wait on the Lord.

I couldn't free my mind of the stray dog we left with her litter of puppies. They were Shag's babies too, and one mirrored him. It was a beautiful puppy and as sweet as they come. Was he starving? I wanted to bring him to Indiana, but I couldn't. I remembered my nine-year-old pet chicken, Granny, and some other pet chickens. What about our pet barn pigeons? I missed Dewey and Queenie, our first pair of pigeons. They were accustomed to my feeding them every day. Were *Glick* (Lucky) and his beautiful hen, Crownie, as lucky now without me? My thoughts swarmed about what I could do with all of these pets as soon as I could get back in the colony.

What about the cats like Springy, Baby, Runt, and all the others? Could they find enough mice since they were taught not to bother the birds? Would they survive?

Would The Elder return once we were gone for awhile?

I still wondered why The Elder took away my good Bible name, Lois, that he had given me when I was four. I had to learn to respond and spell this strange worldly name, Patricia, before we left the colony. Was I not worthy of the good name anymore for some reason? Did he think that once I was cast into this wicked, outside world I wouldn't deserve a good name? I wished I knew the answers. Would I get my Bible name back if I went back into the colony?

I fiercely wanted to do physical work with those in the colony and be in the cotton fields again. I studied hard, but I wanted to do more than just study all day cooped up in Grandma's bedroom. Zealous to memorize God's word, I only hoped I would be accepted back with the colony someday and have grace with God. I decided to try to pick up the pieces and live in my new world to the best of my ability — until then. After all, God allowed me to be moved into this new world. It was not by my choice! People in this world weren't going to change, and I didn't want to be like them. I was the one left to change whatever I could.

I felt what I was taught was right, and I was willing to die for it. I had violated three important things that I was taught never to do: crying, screaming, and getting angry. Would God ever forgive me for those three? I asked Him for forgiveness, but I didn't know if He really had forgiven me. The uncertainty — the lack of assurance of forgiveness — was depressing. All I could do was hope. I began to feel He would forgive me for crying and feeling angry because He did both.

He was angry in the temple, and I remembered the

shortest verse in the Bible, *Jesus wept.* But what about my screaming? It was probably uncalled for. I slowly began crying less each day and didn't feel the urge to scream or be angry any more.

Ich gedanka ich vor en de roda (I thought I was in the red) and an unrighteous person that betrayed the rules of my belief. There is one thing I knew for certain. God loved me even if nobody else did. Although I had sinned and fallen short, He still loved me. My biggest concern was if He would forgive me totally for all my sins He had written in His heavenly record? I surely didn't like the record, but I knew I couldn't go back and change anything.

I found peace in just being able to trust in God, pray to Him, read His Word, and learn all the Bible verses I could. I still worked on the former goal I set in the colony to learn the Bible from cover to cover. I wanted a better understanding of God's Word and also the words of the world. I struggled to do my best to overcome my shyness and blushing. It had to be evil when I turned red because red is a bad color. It felt so sinful. I didn't want to stay in the red.

God put me on this earth to accomplish something. What was it? He allowed me to survive in the colony when I thought I was dying. Why? What could I do now that I was in the world? All I was doing was sitting around waiting . . . for my next dental appointment.

Chapter 7

Teeth and Torture

I went back to the dentist for impressions. The big, bright, hot lights, silver tools, big hands, and floods of memories made me sweat. With his hand in my mouth, Dr. Stamp said, "The infection and swelling are down enough, so I can get impressions today. Then it will take a week to make your dentures." Looking at Mom he continued, "Make an appointment to come back in seven days, and she'll have new teeth."

I would have to come back one more time!

Oh, this impression experience was something else. I gagged and felt like that dentist was truly stuffing my mouth full of everything on his tray. Now I was gagging on more than his fingers and tools. The rubber-base substance he used to make the impressions was like having lots of brown, stiff, stinky dough stuffed in my mouth and half way down my throat. I knew I had to tolerate it if I ever wanted to come out of the bedroom or have anyone see me again. At least there wasn't much pain with this ordeal, only a lot of gagging. When he finished, I left his office ready to count the days until my next trip back for my new teeth. Maybe then life could begin again.

I studied hard that week and felt better emotionally. Finally the appointed day came, and I went to get my new teeth.

The dentist had two rock-hard pieces of flesh colored material laced with rows of popcorn white teeth. He stuffed those two oversized objects into my mouth and said, "Look at me and smile."

He might as well have painted my face with red paint. I could feel the blood rush to my face so quickly that it gave me a headache. The tops of my ears burned from the heat as though he had set them on fire. Slowly I looked up.

"Now smile," he ordered.

My lips felt like skin stretched out to dry. I was to smile? I knew what he meant, but I didn't have much practice and didn't really want to now.

"Come on, come on," the dentist insisted.

When I cracked my lips a bit to please him, he said, "Oh, what nice pearly whites."

Then another huge, rosy flush went across my face. I couldn't wait to get out of his sight and back to Grandma's house. My discomfort got no sympathy from him. I was ushered out of the office with his terse comment, "Call me if you have problems."

When Mom and I went to Uncle Carl's car, he instantly wanted me to smile for him, and I was overcome with another crimson attack of embarrassment. I couldn't talk right, and I bit my tongue when I tried. The ride home was agonizing. I was glad to be back at Grandma's and went straight to the bedroom. My mouth felt so full that I gagged every once in awhile. Fluid ran down my throat, and it was hard to swallow, especially with the already existing knot in my throat.

Everyone wanted to see my mouth full of oversized teeth. I went to the table at supper time thinking I'd be able to eat. What a surprise! Everything I put into my mouth stuck to the dentures. My tongue and lips felt paralyzed. Uncle Carl laughed at me and picked the worst things for me to try to eat. I had to go to the bathroom to dig out what I had put in my mouth.

I deliberately looked in the mirror to see my new teeth and much to my surprise I saw my mouth bulging with appliance-white teeth. It truly felt like I had a stove in my mouth, one big enough to cook a meal on. I couldn't even comfortably eat a bite of anything. My dreams of eating were over instantly, and I drank liquids again that evening.

Teeth and Torture

The next morning I tried eating cereal. The cereal stuck on my new teeth and the roof of my mouth. My knotted throat swelled more during the night. My body was not adjusting well to this foreign appliance!

By the end of the second day my mouth was sore and hurt almost as bad as if I had a toothache. I had to learn how to take these oversized molded teeth out of the giant cavity in my face. That was a task in itself. I brushed them under the faucet just like Grandma did hers, but she was sixty-two and I was only sixteen! *Is this worth it? I can't even eat. How am I to gain any weight? How long will I be on this liquid diet?* My mouth was so sore that it was painful to move my tongue. I was miserable for days. Mom finally called the dentist and made another appointment for a check up and an adjustment.

"Why didn't you come sooner?" Dr. Stamp asked. Then he added, "Your four wisdom teeth have come through and your mouth looks terrible."

How comforting!

Dr. Stamp continued, "I will have to pull your four wisdom teeth today and put you back on an antibiotic. The open sores are infected."

Great! Four more teeth to be pulled and more pills! Where did those four new teeth come from? I thought the teeth-pulling was finished. Now I have to go back on those magical – but sinful little pills – for seven more days.

Having my wisdom teeth pulled was almost worse than when my eyeteeth were pulled. It was a good thing I didn't know what was ahead of me this time or the torture and terror would have raged in my mind all week. Dr. Stamp was short on patience. His idea of enough time for the numbing medicine to take affect was totally different from mine. When he took out the needle-spewing novocaine, he was ready to begin with the clamps.

As he yanked on one of the upper teeth, it felt like my eardrum was being extracted with the tooth. I nearly passed out! He finally realized he had to stop and wait for the novocaine to do its work.

Dr. Stamp jokingly assured me 100% that this would be the last teeth I could possibly ever have pulled. I wasn't impressed by his attempt at humor. Nevertheless it did help me tolerate and endure the pulling of my four wisdom teeth.

After suffering with infections all those years, I was amazed and wondered how it was possible that small pills could take away the infection in my mouth. It seemed like a miracle pill. Was it really sinful to take the tiny pill and not have the pain and infection any more? Was it a sin to feel better? Guilt nagged at me. Yet I told myself, "Don't feel guilty. Mom ordered it and she is really responsible." But was she doing wrong because of me? I didn't like the thought of that either, but I couldn't change it. Then there was the question, "How would I pay for my sins now if I my teeth didn't hurt any more?" I had grown to think that God used my teeth to punish me for my sins.

It was soon time to try eating again, only without any of Uncle Carl's advice. This time I tried very small bites until I could get the hang of these new choppers. That's what my new dentures became as they bit my tongue, the inside of my checks, and the inside of my lips. They proved vicious to the health and well-being of my tender mouth, leaving many scars.

Another trip to the dentist and I had my new dentures realigned, filling in the wisdom teeth voids and tightening the loose fit. Adjusting to my new teeth proved to be quite painful and took a long time. Food has never tasted the same! Even though it took time adjusting to my new false teeth, I never wished my original worn out teeth back again and all the toothaches that had come with them.

After a few more trips to the dentist for minor adjustments where he ground pressuring edges off my dentures, I began to feel thankful I had them. Eventually I became able to control these biters. I ate enough to gain back a couple pounds despite the terrible feeling I had inside.

Homesickness, extreme shyness, my new dentures, and the lump in my throat all prevented me from becoming comfortable talking with people. I began wondering if the lump in my throat was permanent for as I fought to force food down, it often wanted to come right back up. I seriously wondered if I had cancer in my throat and why the antibiotic pills didn't get rid of the knot there. I wasn't about to tell this to anyone for fear I would be forced to see another doctor. I did not want to deal with any more guilt from seeing doctors. I felt hope that God would see me through even with the knot in my throat which felt like a rock that I could choke on at any minute.

What was I to do now? What was in this foreign world for me to learn? What were my real beliefs? What did I not believe? How should I act and eat?

With these struggles now in my heart, this was my prayer, "Lord, help me to find the answers to my many questions. Help me to overcome my shyness and learn how to walk according to your will. Amen."

Patricia Hochstetler

Chapter 8

Soul Searching

It was a new day, majestic and untried. It was early morning when the sun, fresh as a newborn baby, rose in the eastern sky. It was alive — moving — God's creation in motion. I sat on the couch alone with thoughts of soaring like an eagle to watch everything around me instead of flying away like a dove to be at rest. This was an unusual feeling. Maybe there was hope for a new start.

I learned something new every day and began to see that I wasn't as different from other people as I had once thought. I was struggling for my identity. Who am I now that I am stranded in this foreign world? This was a question that haunted me day and night. I had to find answers, and I knew I had to start the search from within me.

When I came here I had lots of faith in God, but I slowly realized that I had too much faith in people. It was an agonizing discovery, but I learned that faith in man can disappoint and destroy. Humans let me down. They scoffed, laughed, and made fun of me. There was no human I could depend on, even the members of my family were changing much too rapidly. The only thing that I had to hold on to was my faith in God, the only solid rock I knew.

When cast into this foreign world, I sat at Grandma's house for weeks waiting, adjusting, and healing. I felt like I was fighting to survive while spinning in the surf of a rough, wild world filled with huge turbulent oceans that sent waves crashing in on my life and my principles. I struggled to make sense of all that had happened in the colony and to contrast that with this real, untamed, circus world I was in. Instead of being surrounded by an extended family, I was in the midst of weird clowns and changing, shiftless maneuvers. The effects and pains were overwhelming. I cried out to God for help. It was hard to imagine Him being in a world as wicked as I was taught this one was, but He was there.

I learned what real faith and trust in God was and how to put it into practice and grow. I was challenged to learn from each experience I faced and to learn how to use stumbling blocks as stepping stones. I continued learning Bible verses and rehearsed the ones I already knew. Now I could concentrate on learning without the interruption of working in the cotton fields. I soon realized, however, that I learned Bible verses more easily if I was busy doing menial tasks.

How life changes! The confidence I had in God's power was as fleeting as a winter's snow. Snow can have such a beautiful pure look. It was the winter of 1964. The purity of the snow was in contrast to the dirt and impurity I felt about this new life. I felt as frozen in time and ice cold to the ways of the worldly people as they looked to me. I was too icy for strangers to get near me. Sometimes I was more like dry ice, and they couldn't see me in the fog.

I needed help! I was thrust to and fro between The Elder and his colony of ever-changing rules and a free-spirited do-it-your-own way of life here in Indiana. I was frustrated, confused, and alone.

I can't ask these worldly heathens for help. I can't even silently signal for them to notice me and my needs because of my confused feelings and exclusive beliefs. We were taught to avoid being seen whenever possible, and the bedroom had become my hideaway. We were taught not to show any emotions. I had learned to cry in secret, but would I ever learn to laugh? I couldn't imagine that possibility, at least never out loud. Laughing was considered foolishness, a really wicked, worldly action according to The Elder.

Sobriety was so engraved in me I couldn't even laugh at funny things. Life was serious and not a laughing matter. We were taught to be sober and vigilant for *the devil was like a roaring lion seeking whom he may devour* (1 Peter 5:8).

Straight and narrow is the path that leads to righteousness, and broad is the way that leads to destruction. (Matthew 7:13,14). In Indiana I saw broad paths and smiles, and everywhere I looked there were things we had been taught were wrong.

Which is right?

I want time . . . time to rethink . . . time to heal emotionally and physically . . . and that's between God and me.

It was all so inconceivable I could hardly hold it in my head. This was truly a world of amazing things. Some of them were good. Some were bad, and I felt I wasn't even to focus on those in this wicked place. Some people actually seemed happier in this world than we were in the colony. Maybe they didn't know about God. I really wondered.

I was taught to always apply The Golden Rule, (Matthew. 7:12), *Therefore, all things whatever ye would that men should do to you, do ye even so to them; for this is the law and the prophets.* To apply the Golden Rule I had to accept people, and the idea that I had to change my feelings toward them to obey God's word seemed inconsistent. But I had to survive in my new world even if for only a short time until I could get back to the colony.

When I was hauled into this strange new world, I knew how to work hard and do whatever work I was told. I learned how to clean at Grandma's house. In fact I learned to dust furniture with a rag for the first time. I was used to bare necessities – a table that we washed and the tops of wood stoves. I was not accustomed to cleaning shinning mirror-like furniture, pictures, the nick knacks setting around, and smooth shinny floors that need to be mopped and waxed. Our floors were old worn boards. A broom was our only sweeper, and this noisy tank that we pulled was really strange. There seemed to be more dust in Indiana than in Mississippi, or maybe I had more time to notice it. I missed cleaning the black, sooty globes on our oil lamps and even the stinky chicken roost.

With each pulse of life in my new world, I felt God's help. I knew He loved and cared about me even in a place where I couldn't understand how He could be present. It was hard to imagine Him in this worldly environment, but I knew I could never have survived here by myself. I needed, trusted, and appreciated Him more with each passing day.

I wished God would make time stand still for me like He did for Joshua. I wanted time so I could catch up and understand what was happening. I longed to grasp on to how people in this new world lived, thought, and worked. Of course it didn't happen, and I knew it was up to me to do whatever it took for me to learn how to cope with my situation.

One place to start was in writing. I didn't know how to make the small letters like the worldly people did. In the colony we had been taught to make them like the capitals only smaller. So while I was in limbo, I decided to learn how to make all the lower case letters the new way. I copied them from books, and if I was unsure I asked Grandma. She seemed to like helping me, and I practiced until I was able to write them well.

I realized an amazing truth for the first time. I would become free only when I set myself free! I wanted to be free to believe, accept, or reject what I faced as I felt God would want. Nobody else recognized if I was free or bound. For days my lips remained as quiet as my thoughts. I had a good excuse because my mouth was full of new teeth.

I could visualize the raging rivers I had to cross if I hoped to survive. I could imagine the rugged and steep mountains I still had to climb beyond today. These rivers I had to cross seemed cold, deep, and wide, and the mountains straight up. It looked impossible. All I could do was to trust God to help me get to the other side. My brain was so busy processing the unfamiliar that I could hear and yet not perceive some things because there was no point of reference. I saw things, but I felt like a sheer curtain was hung over my eyes and skewed how I perceived many things. I heard and saw things vaguely and only later did I *really* see and perceive them. I wondered why I didn't see and understand it all the first time. This soul searching was having a permanent effect on who I would become both then and now.

Most things I saw and heard put a big question mark in my mind. Are they right or wrong? Valid or not? If I accept the new things, what would be the results? Would I be convicted for sin? If I didn't say yes to the new, how would I be perceived? For years I have had to choose among thousands of these new things. Even today I continue to find things unfamiliar to me that most people grew up with and take for granted.

During this time of adjustment I felt battered by adversity, and prayed, "Oh, Lord give me a rest. I need a refuge and place to hide. My life feels consumed with grief and misery." I wanted out of this new world. I felt like I was bleeding internally and hurting with invisible aches.

I tried to focus on the familiar that I saw in my mom, my brother, my sister and everything in the sky. I watched the clouds and sun each day and the moon and stars at night whenever nature allowed. But my mind was hostage by memories of the colony and The Elder's teachings.

Peter's writing described my situation, "A double minded person is unstable in all his thinking."

There was far too much uncertainty in my world. The days and months of soul searching convinced me of one thing: God is my refuge and strength, a help in time of trouble.

But the knowledge of where I fit eluded me.

Patricia Hochstetler

Chapter 9

Traumatic Experiences

I rested on the Sabbath and even a few days after. I gave myself time to think, evaluate, and regroup. If only I could go back to the colony now, I wouldn't have those horrible toothaches. But to get there I must. . . . The list seemed hard and long.

Although nothing was ever said in my presence, I believe Grandma insisted that Uncle Carl stay at Aunt Marie's home as long as he kept drinking. "It's not a good example for the children," Grandma told Mom when she asked about Uncle Carl's absence from the house.

With Uncle Carl gone there was no more teasing, scolding, and scoffing all day. The quiet, peaceful days felt good. Determined to never get out of control and cry as before, I prayed, "Lord, help me now. Show me what you want me to do. Amen." My heart cried as I struggled for composure. I read more in Psalms which lifted my spirit.

I was free to roam the house, and on this morning I went to the kitchen and ate a bowl of cereal. My new dentures felt better and most of the sores in my mouth and on my gums had healed. The infections were gone. After brushing my teeth, the mirror revealed I even looked more alive and normal. A step on Grandma's scales and it showed I had gained two pounds. I felt better.

Nevertheless the world in Elkhart was still so full of the unknown and unimaginable for me. In spite of less stress with Uncle Carl out of the house and improved health which I begrudgingly credited to the dentist and his sinful pills, I still remembered the words of The Elder. He often preached,

"You are no match for the outside world, and you will surely perish outside our colony." This was almost a sure death promise from God's servant, a man God spoke to daily. I was positive God would allow somebody to cross my path to test my faith in Him. Then they would kill me just as The Elder predicted. I was ready and waiting for that time. Uncle Carl proved to be the cruelest person I encountered so far, but I was certain the real test was yet to come. Until that time life went on.

I spent the day deciding on what would be the first thing I could do to help myself be more comfortable around people — until my test of faith came. My first goal was to overcome shyness. If I could do that, I would not turn red when people said "hi" to me or asked me a question. I would know how to answer if I blushed and they asked why I was blushing. If I achieved this goal, I might be able to master a second goal and get a job. My third goal would be to save money for a bus ticket and go back to Mississippi. I determined to do my best and begin practicing to overcome shyness and blushing when people came to the house. The opportunity came sooner than I expected.

The next day Dick Clemens came to visit Mom and Grandma. Mom and Dad knew Dick and his wife, Rosa, before we disappeared from Indiana. This was about to be my first practice. When Dick knocked on the back door, instead of running to the bedroom as usual I stayed in the kitchen. I didn't know him, and as he talked I went through agony and blushed over and over. I was a world away from my comfort zone. But I survived this first time, and it helped me toward my goal. It took weeks before I could see him again and not turn crimson shades. Other people kept streaming in to visit. Some seemed real nice, but talking with each new person was like I had a battle to be won. That wouldn't change for a few more years.

I kept asking myself, "When will I meet the person The Elder said would test my faith?"

The next week Fred was the first one home after work. He popped into the kitchen and we sat at the table eating a snack. "Do you really like your job?" I asked.

"Yes, but I feel like I'm not working much until I lift the fifty pound bags of potatoes," Fred admitted with a smile. "I'm not sure I work enough peeling potatoes and taking trash out to get the pay they give me, but I like it. It's nothing like hoeing and picking cotton!"

"Do you think I would like working there?"

"You might," Fred answered, "but they aren't hiring now." He immediately recognized my disappointment and quickly added, "I gotta go now because there's a bunch of boys planning to play baseball in the empty lot behind Grandma's house."

"Is it right to play like that?" I questioned. "Do you know how to play baseball?"

"I don't know about right or wrong," he mumbled. "I don't know how to play it, but I plan to try and maybe I can learn how." He hurried out the back door.

Did Fred even think about how we were taught to work and not ever play? In a few minutes Fred returned to Grandma's enclosed back porch area and poked his head in the kitchen door.

"Trish, come here! Come, look at this cigarette." Fred quietly whispered and beckoned. "The boys gave it to me, and they gave me these matches too. Here, I'll light it and you try taking in a puff of air through it."

"No! No! That's like Uncle Carl's stinky things," I protested.

"Oh, come on, Trish, try it once . . . only once in your life," Fred begged. "Hurry up before Joan gets off the school bus or Mom and Grandma get home from work."

"You smoked a cigarette?" I asked in disbelief.

"I didn't really smoke it. I only took one puff. Come on and try it," Fred pleaded as he lit the cigarette and demonstrated how to inhale. "Like this . . . you put your mouth on this end and draw in air through this thing. It's a filter so the smoke is not as strong. Let all the air out of your lungs like this." He exhaled.

"Now draw a big breath through the cigarette filter."

He inhaled — but not through the filter.

"Breathe it all the way into your lungs without stopping. No tiny breaths . . . only one big long one. Here, now try it! Hurry and do it quick. Come on! It won't kill you. I did it. Like this!"

He put the cigarette close to his mouth.

"You aren't breathing it in like you told me to do," I was quick to point out. "You're only holding your mouth close to the end. Your lips aren't even touching it."

"I'm only showing you how. I did it outside with my mouth tight on it, and I want you to try it," Fred begged holding the cigarette to my mouth. "Just do it quick now . . . right now. You don't even need to touch the cigarette with your hands . . . only with your lips. Now take a big breath of air all the way into your lungs. That's all there is to it! Come on, Trish, try it!"

He put the cigarette to my lips. I emptied my lungs and took one big breath of air in through the filter end of the cigarette, and I choked . . . and choked! Coughing and gagging I couldn't get my breath. I had tried it!

Fred grinned and said, "I just wanted to see if it affected you like it did me. I did the same thing and still feel bad from it. Are you okay?"

"No!" I answered choking, and I sat down on the steps. "I'm terribly dizzy and feel sick. Why did you do that to me?"

"I wanted you to know how horrible cigarettes really are," Fred seriously claimed as he dashed out the door to play ball.

It all happened in seconds. Feeling dazed I went to my bedroom and lay on my bed thinking, *why did I ever let Fred talk me into something foolish like that?* From the smell of Uncle Carl's cigarettes, I knew it must be horrible. This experience made me think of how Eve let the snake talk her into taking a bite of the apple in Bible days. Why did I ever do it? Would I somehow pay for this evil? I was disappointed in myself, and felt guilty and ashamed. I prayed, "My Lord God, please forgive me for this sin. Please forgive me now. Help me not to do anything like that again," I moaned.

I have never tried another cigarette, and Fred does not smoke either.

I felt bad all that evening. Mom, Joan, and Grandma came home and I never told them what had happened. I wondered if Fred was headed down the wrong path with those heathen boys. I felt determined to never get caught up in anything like that again.

A few days later when I knew the boys were going to be playing, I went to the backyard and hid behind some bushes along the back fence. I was curious and I watched to see how this baseball stuff went. It was amazing. One boy threw the white ball. Another boy hit it and then ran and flopped on the ground while the others watched. I didn't get it. It looked like foolish horseplay to me or like a bunch of young cows in the pasture just before a rain when they liked to run and kick up their heels. It wasn't so bad until the ball was hit in the bushes near me, and I was discovered. Some boys came to the fence and talked to me. My face turned shades of red and the boys asked me what was wrong.

"Why do you wear a long dress like that? What are you hiding under it? We like the short dresses," one boy snarled. "Why are you wearing that tailed turban on your head? You look funny, girl." He laughed a crude laugh. As he headed back to the ball field, he yelled, "Go home, you dunce!"

I had no answers they accepted, and I went into the house knowing I did not belong out there. I saw that Fred didn't know how to play ball, but the boys were trying to teach him. After dark that evening Fred said to me, "I felt sorry for you the way those boys acted and talked to you."

"They don't treat you that way," I responded. "Why do you think they laughed at me and acted like that?"

"I don't know. Maybe it's because my clothes don't look as different as yours," Fred said with a serious look. "It wasn't very nice of them."

It was not long until Joan coaxed, "Trish, will you visit my school one day to see what it's like? But don't wear your head covering or the students will make fun of you. Just leave your hair down straight like after it's washed or braid it. And wear a plain navy shirt and white blouse. Come and try it."

"Let me think about it."

Joan struggled to adjust to some things at school. Often she became ill on days she felt unable to do what teachers ordered like giving an oral report. Wearing gym shorts and taking showers in physical education class also proved to be tough for her. She frequently accepted detention for not bringing her gym suit.

One night I finally said, "Joan, I decided to try going to school with you. Is tomorrow okay?"

"Sure is, but we have gym. It's horrible," Joan announced. "I'll just forget my gym suit, and we can sit together."

The next morning I boarded the school bus with Joan and this was quite a noisy experience. Would the greyhound bus to Mississippi be like that? We arrived at Concord Junior High School, Joan showed me her locker, and we dashed to her seventh grade classroom just before a buzzer sounded. The day was off to a noisy start.

I braved this adventure, and did I ever get a strong dose of practicing my first goal! It seemed like I spent the day blushing and blushing. I met the bus driver, children on the bus, classmates, teachers, and the principal, Mr. Sweisberger. I ate lunch with Joan in a huge cafeteria. We had to eat really fast, but I had no appetite and only ate a few bites of soft foods because I still couldn't chew well with my new teeth. I wondered what the school children would think if they knew that I had false teeth. I would never tell a soul, and I knew that I was the only child in the place with dentures. I couldn't believe the size of the lunch area, how many children, and how loud they sounded. After lunch I was shocked when Joan went with a bunch of girls and tried to dance to music. "Come on, Trish, try dancing!" Joan pleaded. "It's fun, and I'll teach you how."

"Not a chance! I will not try that," I firmly declared. "Why would I want to jerk my body around like they are?

What's fun about that?"

"Please don't tell Mom about me dancing, okay? Please!" Joan sheepishly begged.

I could see Joan had advanced far more into worldly things than I had ever imagined or was prepared to attempt. That was okay because I had plans to return to Lael Colony. I certainly would never have fit in the public school.

I didn't tell anybody about Joan dancing and I never let her know that Fred had coaxed me into trying a cigarette. Her next class after lunch was physical education. Joan was reprimanded and given detention for not bringing her gym suit, and we sat on the side and watched. After their work out all the girls stormed into the shower room. What a shock this was for me! Girls stripped all their clothes off and ran into the showers as though they thought nothing of it. I had never seen nudity before. I turned my head away. Naturally I blushed again. This was too much. I was in shock!

"Joan, no wonder you don't want to go to this class," I said. "I wouldn't want to go either." I felt sorry for her. She was forced by the state to go to school and to be in gym class or be punished. By the end of the day I was exhausted and blushed out completely. I enjoyed listening in her classes. I would have liked studying and learning.

Once school started Aunt Marie insisted that Joan let her cut her hair to shoulder length. She was determined to cut my hair too, but I refused. After all, I had plans to return to Lael Colony. One day I had just washed my hair and Aunt Marie was there at the house.

"Please let me brush your hair," she begged. "I've never worked with hair as long as yours. It's wavy and beautiful, and you can sit on it. I like it. I want to feel it, brush it, and braid it for you. Please let me."

"Okay, if it means that much to you," I agreed. "You can brush it, but don't cut my hair!"

"I won't. I won't," Aunt Marie promised with a smile. "I'm not like Uncle Carl. You can trust me. He's mean to you isn't he? Humm!" There was a long awkward silence! "That's why he's staying at my house now. I'm tough and can handle him and his drunken stupors. You feel tense. Now just relax and I'll brush your hair. I'm a hair stylist you know. I brush, comb, and cut hair all the time. That's my job. Come on relax! I see your hair has some split ends that are unhealthy. Those ends should be cut off for your hair to grow well. Can I trim them?"

"No, I don't want my hair cut," I protested. "It has grown for sixteen years without being trimmed or cut, and it will be fine. Just don't cut it."

"Well, things were different when you lived in that cult," she responded arrogantly. "Now you're free and all the things you've gone though with your teeth might have put you under stress and caused the ends to split. And the split ends should be trimmed off. Mary, what do you think? See these split ends."

Mom looked and said, "Oh, there's only a couple of split ends. It's not a big deal."

"What do split ends look like?" I asked. "Can I see them?"

"See these two split ends," Aunt Marie pointed out. "A half inch trimmed off your hair would get rid of the split ends, and it will grow better."

"Just pull the two hairs out," I implored. "Don't cut them off!"

"Okay, just relax! I'll braid your hair," Aunt Marie muttered rolling her big brown eyes. "Relax! Just relax!"

What had I gotten myself into? With Mom sitting nearby I tried to relax. Before I knew what was happening Aunt Marie said, "See that wasn't bad. It didn't hurt, and you didn't even know it."

"Know what?" I asked noticing Mom's silent but telling face after she looked up from reading the paper. "What's wrong?"

Aunt Marie held out a long braid. I knew instantly it had to be mine, and it was too late to run. My thoughts froze for a moment. Then I wondered, *Why did I trust her? This is not like the trustworthy people I grew up with.* Who could I trust in my new world? I could trust God; I knew He keeps

His word. I felt betrayed and wondered how I could explain my cut hair when I went back into Lael Colony. This made me sick to my stomach and left me without words to express myself. Half my hair was gone.

"Well, your hair needed to be cut, and that's the only way it would get done," Aunt Marie mumbled as she unbraided what hair she had left on my head. "Now I must trim around the bottom to smooth the jagged ends."

I felt deceived and trapped. Mom was also surprised and speechless. My hair was cut off at my shoulder blades, and Aunt Marie had no words of apology. She soon popped out the door and went home. This was a tough lesson. My head felt light and after three days my neck became sore and stayed sore for weeks. The weight adjustment seemed to make a big difference on my head, and my short braids pinned up did not fill out my head covering anymore. I felt like crying, but I wouldn't let myself. Tears would not change what had happened.

"It was wrong for Aunt Marie to make you believe you could trust her," Mom said sincerely. "She did what she wanted. Patricia, remember your hair will grow out again."

I felt caught in a right or wrong issue because I had been taught it was wrong to cut my hair. Nothing could make it right even if it grew back. Cutting my hair felt wrong to me, and it rattled my emotions. I suffered with hurt and regret that I had trusted her and allowed this to happen. My hair didn't fill out the covering and certainly wouldn't grow fast enough to do so before I planned to return to Mississippi. Now I would need to put a handkerchief or some kind of filler inside my head covering.

In time after all these traumatic experiences I began to feel better physically. But as long as God allowed me to live, I awaited the chance to fulfill my first three goals: overcome shyness, get a job, and earn enough money to get a bus ticket and return to Mississippi to live in Lael Colony with my Amish-Jewish family.

Time was my only hope.

Patricia Hochstetler

Chapter 10

Learning on My First Job

Since God allowed me so many second chances in life, He must have a reason for it. I certainly had no idea why. I decided to try to do my best and see what good things I could find in my new world. Because I had faith that God allowed all this to happen, I would wait for Him to show me what He had in mind. Maybe there was some kind of hope for me in this new world.

One sunny autumn day I confided in Mom. "There are three goals I have set for myself. I want to overcome my shyness, get a job, and return to Mississippi."

Mom listened intently as I continued. "I can eat better now, and I feel better. Several weeks ago Uncle Carl said 'if you lose any more weight you'll blow away like a leaf in the wind.' So I weighed myself on Grandma's scales. I've gained two pounds and now weigh 88. Do you think I'll get back to 99 pounds like I used to be?"

"Since you have new teeth now and the soreness is better, you might get back to your usual weight," Mom encouraged. "I believe you've been homesick and that can cause weight loss. I hope you can get over your shyness and blushing. That would make it easier for you on a job in the public. I'll start watching the newspaper for a job for you. I don't think you can wear your long colony clothes in the public without a lot of questions. I'll make you a new skirt and blouse in case you get a job. Once you make enough money for a bus ticket, I'll go with you to Mississippi."

Mom was devastated when we arrived in Indiana and she found out that all she had to wear were the clothes on her back. Somehow the box packed with her clothes had been left behind in Mississippi. So shortly after we arrived Mom made a shorter gray skirt for herself.

She made a couple of mid-calf length skirts for Joan before she started school. By now I had become accustomed to seeing Mom and Joan in those different clothes. Did I want to wear them? Not really! But I did want to return to Mississippi. That meant getting a job and that forced a change in my clothes.

Mom had made me a navy blue skirt gathered at the waist and mid-calf length. It was about eight inches shorter and much lighter weight than my colony dress. She also made a white, long sleeved blouse like I wore in the colony but without the blue ribbon trim. She suggested I could also wear my old blouses with the navy blue ribbon trim. Mom cut the legs off of a pair of my ankle-length colony underpants and shortened one of my old slips. She left the short sleeves in my slip, so everything at the top felt the same. I wore knee high socks to cover my legs. This felt strange, but I accepted it.

I went out in the yard to rake leaves and met some of Grandma Long's neighbors. Her cousin, Eva Hess, lived next door. My great Aunt Hess' body was round and plump much like Grandma Miller's. She always welcomed me and treated me kindly, but she asked me mountains of questions. I didn't like her many questions because I didn't know what to say most of the time. This pressured me and I chose to visit her less because of her many questions.

During the next week Mom called excitedly, "Patricia, look here in the newspaper. There's a job for baby-sitting a three year old. You can do that, can't you?" Mom asked and then read the ad to me.

"I don't know. I've never been around any babies or small children. What would I do?"

"It's not hard to care for only one child," Mom assured me. "You just meet their needs like helping them get dressed, fixing their meals, and watching them so they don't get hurt."

I listened carefully as she continued.

"I believe you can do it. You need something to do if

you want to make enough money to buy a bus ticket to Mississippi. I'll call and inquire about the job. Okay?"

"Okay." I sheepishly agreed and waited while Mom made the call.

"The child's a boy," Mom said excitedly after she was off the phone. "They want the house cleaned and some laundry done. You can do that. I told the lady we were from an Amish background and didn't have transportation. She said she'd pick you up on Monday morning and bring you home on Friday evening. They have a bedroom you could have by yourself. I asked if I could go with you the first day or two and she agreed. She wanted to know when you could start and I told her next week on my two days off. Are you ready to try it?"

"If you go with me, I will." I said wondering, *how is this possible?*

"The lady wants to pick us up tomorrow evening so we can meet her boy and her husband and show us around her house before she hires you. Be ready when I get off work and we'll go with the lady," Mom ordered.

The next evening we went with the lady and saw her home and the room where I would stay all week. I met her husband and their son, Bobby. He was an adorable little boy. She explained what she wanted done, how it was to be done, and the schedule for doing it. She hired me. I didn't know whether to be happy or scared to death. It was really a mixture of both.

"Now you have a job," Mom announced when we got back home. "You'll need a second dress so you have something to wear when you wash the other one. I don't have much money, so we'll go to a Goodwill Store. That's a place where they sell used clothing. We'll see if they have a plain navy or gray dress that fits you."

This was all new to me, and I had no idea what was happening, but I wanted to go to Mississippi.

Grandma took Mom and me to the Goodwill Store. We found a plain and simple charcoal gray dress for one dollar. It was pleated at the waist, fairly long, and with a wide hem.

"I can let the hem out and make it longer," I suggested.

"I'll get this beige bra for you . . . something different from your homemade ones."

"I don't need it, Mom. My homemade one is fine." I didn't really want anything different.

Mom insisted and bought the dress and bra.

Once home I took out the wide hem which lengthened the dress to mid-calf. I tried the dress on and wasn't sure if I could adjust to a dress with a waist and belt. All I had worn most of my life was our heavy, straight, sack-type, jumper dresses. These lightweight short dresses didn't feel or seem right.

I felt like my eyes and mind were traveling 50 or even 100 m.p.h. trying to catch up with all the things I had to learn in this new world. I had to talk with people so I could know more of what they meant and then do my new job right. I discovered the newspaper for the first time. I was impressed by the many informative things that I had never heard about before. When Grandma watched the news on television in the evening, I began watching and listening. This suddenly opened my mind to many more things.

I had learned to clean, dust, sweep the carpet and linoleum, and mop the floors in Grandma's house, so cleaning a house seemed easy. Washing clothes was also easy, but I still didn't know if caring for a child would be easy.

The time came to find out, and Mom went with me on that first day. The lady seemed nice and had a schedule ready. Bobby was happy to see us. Mom showed me how to dress him, give him breakfast, show him stuff to play with, talk and read to him, give him lunch, and lay him down for a nap. She showed me how to clean the house each day and how to do laundry. The second day I did it myself and she watched. By Tuesday evening I felt I could do fine by myself and Grandma came and took Mom home.

All went well the rest of the week, and the lady took me home Friday evening for the weekend. Before I got out of the car, she paid me in cash. This was the first time I had ever been handed money. It was money – real money – that I had earned. Was it still wrong for me to touch or have money? The Elder said it was evil. Lurking in the back of my mind was the thought that maybe if I was saving the money for a bus ticket back to God's people in Mississippi that would make it all right.

I rushed into the house and gave Mom all of my money. It felt good to get it out of my hands.

"I promise I'll save it for your bus ticket to Mississippi," Mom said. "When there's enough money, I'll go with you."

I anxiously waited for that day.

I now had my first job established. I was happy about it and like Fred, I didn't feel like I was working. We were used to hard work and this seemed like doing nothing. I could call Mom in the evenings after work. She encouraged me a lot and told me how to do things whenever I had questions. This was the first time for me to ever be completely away from all my family. It felt strange and perhaps a little frightening.

During the day I was alone with three-year-old Bobby. I was in charge and felt responsible for everything. While he slept, I read my Bible. The view across Simington Lake from their backyard was beautiful. I had never seen or been around a lake like that, and at first this all felt scary. With Bobby's company and help I adjusted well. I also learned where every-thing was and did my work early each day and had the rest of the day with him.

Bobby was a great teacher! I learned so much from him. My life in the colony was void of a natural childhood. There had been no exposure to toys or typical, normal childish behavior. He was my teacher. He taught me how to play peek-a-boo and hide and seek. For the first time, I saw and played with simple things like blocks, trucks, cars, and all kinds of toys. Most importantly he taught me how to laugh and love, to give and receive hugs and tiny kisses. He taught me how to show love to a person. I read and learned nursery rhymes for the first time. I really enjoyed relating to this tiny person. He was so much better than a baby doll. He was real and I loved him.

I liked my quiet Mondays through Fridays away from Grandma's home. Being there on the weekends was enough. I began to enjoy freedom, responsibility, and commitment.

I enjoyed every minute of my baby-sitting job until one nice warm, autumn day my boss came home from work on her lunch hour. Bobby and I were in the yard enjoying the sun and each other. We ran to greet his mom until she shouted, "What's going on? Bobby is not to be outside without shoes on! Trisha, you should know that."

I cringed and quickly took Bobby inside and put shoes on his feet. His mom went back to work, and Bobby and I went outside until his nap time. As Bobby napped, I tried to figure out why she was upset with him outside barefoot. It was cool in the morning but had warmed up to a comfortable temperature by noon. There were some evenings I had sat with the family when they were all outside barefoot and in swimsuits. I didn't understand why this day was so different. It seemed she was pleased with my work and me before this incident.

On Friday my boss paid me. As she took me home, she informed me that I was fired for letting Bobby go outside barefoot. This crushed me. I had gone barefoot most of my life and didn't think anything about Bobby being barefoot on a nice day. She said my house cleaning, laundry work, and the relationship I had developed with Bobby was very satisfactory, but she had to let me go. I was crushed!

She went into Grandma's house with me and told my mom what had happened. She said she couldn't take a chance of worrying about Bobby while she worked. She said she had a daycare lined up for Bobby starting Monday and didn't need me anymore. After she left I told Mom exactly what had happened. Mom explained what fired meant and that some people are very particular about having shoes on their children unless they're swimming. She encouraged me to not worry about it because I did the best I could. It was hard to think of not seeing Bobby any more. He had taught me so much – how to use the word love and to show what it meant – how to laugh and play. I missed his simple and innocent ways.

A few days after I was fired Mom came into the bedroom to talk. "Patricia, you've earned more than enough money for a bus ticket to Mississippi."

"If I made enough money for a ticket, I'm ready to go anytime," I said eagerly. "Whenever you can get off, I'm ready."

"I don't know when or if I can get off work. It's starting to get colder, and they won't be as busy at the drive in. Maybe my boss will give me a vacation." We waited.

Winter came and I had my first view of snow blanketing the ground. The white snow glistened with bright clear glittering sparkles in the sunlight. How beautiful and pure it seemed. Since I was out of a job, I had time to enjoy this white covering. It says in the Bible that God can wash sin as white as snow. How can He do that? Then The Elder said my mud doll was a graven image and that meant I broke the Ten Commandments. How could God possibly make that sin as white as snow? Then I remembered that all things are possible with God. Without The Elder here to guide me I had to trust God to guide me because I certainly didn't know what to do.

I had no real heavy winter coat and could not stay out in the snow for long, but I found myself packing snow into a ball in my hands and eating it. Although unfamiliar, snow seemed almost as nice as the blue sky, fleecy clouds, and bright stars. But the snow was on the ground where I could touch it.

Fred and some neighbor boys rolled big snowballs in Grandma's side yard, and I enjoyed watching them from inside the house. They stacked some snowballs on top of each other, put a face on the top ball, and called it a snowman. Whoa! It was much larger than my mud doll. Was that what the Bible called an idol? Was it sinful to make it? I was sure that it was. I vowed not to attempt making one until I knew more.

I liked the white cottony snow blanket that God put on the ground. This snow lesson and the cold temperatures broadened my views of God's creation. But it also left a lot of new unanswered questions.

Maybe this new world wasn't so bad after all.

Chapter 11

Shattered Hopes

Mom was surprised when she received a letter from her brother, Uncle Zack. The news we received was even more shocking. He left the colony! He was not dumped like Joseph. He was not excommunicated like Mom. He was not forced out like we were. He left because he wanted to. He found a job and worked for some Mennonite people who had recently moved into the Clarksdale, Mississippi, area.

About that same time we received a letter from the veterans hospital in Biloxi, Mississippi. Dad had been there for six months and had received extensive, experimental shock treatments. He was going to be released in the next few months if he had a place to live.

This sent emotions flying! I was excited. I was scared.

Fred was decisive. He was not even going to try to deal with Dad again. "I'm outta here," he announced and quickly quit his job, bought a bus ticket to Mississippi, and left to join Uncle Zack.

My friend – my co-worker – my brother was gone!

Joan was absorbed in school and didn't seem to care.

Mom was in shock. There were too many unanswered questions.

Grandma was extremely excited for her son would be coming home.

This turmoil and the knowledge that Fred was moving back to Mississippi made me more anxious to return.

I was elated a short time later when we received a letter from Fred. He was sharing a house with Uncle Zack and working for some of the Mennonite people that Uncle Zack had discovered.

"Patricia, if I can get off work, maybe we should take our bus trip to Mississippi now," Mom suggested.

"I'm ready to go."

Mom got some time off work and we left for Mississippi. This experience was unforgettable. I took cult clothes along but wore the navy skirt and white blouse Mom had made for me.

I knew nothing of the segregation in the south. I sat where I was not supposed to and at a bus station I drank from a water fountain that I was not supposed to. People stared at me as if I had committed a crime. I didn't know why until a man at the bus station showed us signs. The restrooms and things were marked blacks and whites. This seemed unreal, and I didn't understand it at all.

When we arrived at the Clarksdale bus station, Allen Williams, the plantation manager, and his wife, Ethyl, met us and took us to where Fred and Zack lived. Allen asked how Dad's mental condition was and where he was. He informed us again that when Dad was released he was not allowed on the cotton plantation. That reminder was painful, but I could understand Allen's decision.

I was glad to see Fred, but it seemed strange for Zack to be speaking freely with us again. He had to use a *meiding* (shunning) on us before, and it was wonderful to see and feel the change.

My goal was to see if I could return to live in Lael Colony. Mom was not allowed in there because The Elder had excommunicated her, but I was considered a gray area because I was forced to leave with my family. I had a chance to visit with my grandfather, aunts, and uncles. I had walked a mile into Lael Colony to ask my big question. "May I come back and live with the colony, even if it's in a tent in the woods?"

Grandpa informed me that I could not. Since my parents were not in the colony, they did not want me living in the nearby woods or plan to work with them in the cotton fields. His words shattered all the hopes and dreams I had had for months. What was I going to do now?

After this experience Mom and I went to Columbus, Mississippi, to see the Abraham Schrock family. All these cousins had been excommunicated about eight years earlier when the colony was still in Tennessee. Aunt Lydia, Grandma Miller's sister and Abraham's wife, had died from a burst gallbladder, and we had not seen the family for all those years. It felt strange to speak with Abraham whom The Elder had called "the bear" and "the bull of Bashan." He had told us not to let him in our houses even if it was raining pitch forks. Yet here we were — The Elder's rejects — together at their house eating, talking, and enjoying each other.

I liked talking to Dorothy and Josephine, both a bit older than me. I knew I could not live in their house because it was still too full of children. There were fifteen in their family. Three of the older girls had moved out and lived in a mobile home in Starksville, Mississippi. Maybe I could live with them. They would understand me far more than the Indiana people. So Mom and I went to visit the three, Frieda, Edith, and Dena. My big question, "May I live with you?" was soon answered. I saw it was not possible for me to live with them in their small, mobile home. They also had other sisters who wanted to live with them.

This exhausted all the possibilities of my return to live in Mississippi. I was depressed. I would have to return to Indiana without hope of living with any people from our colony. There was one more possibility however. Mom and I went to visit Fred one more time and to meet the Mennonites he worked for in Clarksdale.

"Fred, do you think there is any chance I could clean house, baby-sit, or do any kind of work for the Mennonites. Would they let me stay with them?" I asked.

"No!" Fred replied emphatically. "You only work for them if you're running big machines. The ladies do all their own work in the house."

"Do you really like them and enjoy working for them?"

"I sure do! The Mennonite people are great. They feed me good, and I really like the work," Fred replied with a chuckle. "I feel like I'm working again. It's not like the restaurant work. When I'm eighteen, they'll train me to run the big earth movers, and I'll like that."

As Fred and I chatted, I could tell he had changed a lot. He laughed and he seemed more relaxed than I had seen him in many years. His eyes didn't twitch anymore, and he seemed happy, and I was happy for him. Fred then confided in me as he often did and said, "Remember that cigarette I made you try and how terrible it was?"

"Yes, I certainly do!" I growled and wrinkled my face.

"Well, I had a chance to try beer, alcohol, and whiskey. Never try that stuff. It's horrible. It made me so sick that I wished I'd die, but I couldn't," Fred warned. "I vomited all over and lay in it all night unable to move. I got sicker than I've ever been in my life. Never try it! Never!"

"Don't worry. I sure don't plan to ever try it," I quickly snapped. "That's horrible! I'll take your word for it. What did you do then?"

"I lay until I got well enough to go again," Fred said regretfully.

"Fred, what do you think I should do now that I found out I can't go back into the colony, and I haven't found any place to live and work in Mississippi?"

"Well, I never could see why you wanted back into the colony. I lived to get out of there. Now I'm free!" Fred answered sincerely. "I guess you were always more sincere about doing what was right than I was. Have you ever thought about there might be other ways that are right in this world besides what we grew up to believe? Think about it! These Mennonite people are nice, good, and sincere people. I've learned more here than I ever learned in our colony. Give yourself a chance and some time to think about it."

"I will think about what you said," I assured Fred, "and I'm glad you're happy here."

"You don't need to expect me back in Indiana," Fred said with a voice of confidence. "Do you know when Dad's getting out of the hospital?"

"I'm not sure," I whispered. "I know he's terribly angry

that Carl had Shag put to sleep. He says it should never have been done. What do you think will happen?" I asked.

"I can only guess!" Fred nodded with a worried look. "When you get back to Indiana, why don't you go to Mr. Checkley and tell him you would be happy to do my job? He might hire you. Then you and Mom could work at the same place."

"I will," I muttered, "but I don't really know what to do since my plans to live here have been shattered."

"I know you'll make it one way or another," Fred said with that determined look in his eyes. "If you and I could build a chimney when we were younger, we can do anything."

I had to leave for the north without any hope of living with people from Lael Colony or in Mississippi. We bid farewell and Mom and I returned to Indiana. Now I knew! My hopes were shattered. Everything I wanted for my future was lost. I didn't know what to plan for or expect. Mom and I never said much on the trip home.

Once back in Indiana I went to apply for Fred's previous job, and Mr. Checkley had already hired somebody. However he did hire me as a dishwasher, and I walked to work with Mom. The dishwashing job kept me busier than baby-sitting. When I caught up on washing dishes, I had to wash lettuce heads and tear them apart for garnishing sandwiches. I liked this job at Checkley's Drive-In and working with Mom.

Would I ever really find a place in this Indiana world where I will be happy? I had my doubts.

Patricia Hochstetler

Chapter 12

Grandma's Church

The minute Grandma set foot out of bed on Sunday mornings she would ask, "Will you go to church with me this morning? It's only for one hour. If you go, I'll skip Sunday school and just take you to church, okay?"

"What's Sunday school?" I asked, "and what's church? What's the difference?"

"Sunday school is one hour where we meet to learn more about Jesus," Grandma explained. People meet together in different age groups and each group meets in a separate room. You'd be in the high school group." I had always gone to Sabbath meetings to learn about God. I didn't understand why they couldn't all meet together to learn about Him.

Grandma saw the confused look on my face and continued talking. "The actual church service is one hour where everybody sits together and listens to the preacher's sermon. All you would need to do is sit one hour and listen. That's all! Will you go this time, please? You now have your new teeth and look so good. Come on just try it and you'll be blessed." *Blessed or cursed?* The Elder referred to all the 'worldly churches' as the houses of the devil. I was comforted by the fact that I had kept my Sabbath yesterday in the bedroom all day. I rested, read the Bible, and prayed.

Already dressed in my long navy skirt and my white blouse trimmed with blue ribbon, I watched Grandma excitedly scramble around getting ready for church. She fastened a bright pin on her flowered dress, and she used two pearl-ended spear-like pins to hold on her veiled hat.

Grandma's chubby high heels made a click-clack sound

She turned to me, "Okay! Now we're all set, Patricia. Let's eat and you're going to church with me this morning. I made arrangements for somebody to take my place teaching Sunday school."

Now what was I into? I hadn't said I would even go, and she found somebody to teach her class, a class that she had taught for 30 years. I was silent as we all sat at the table and ate cereal as Grandma always insisted we do on Sunday mornings.

"Patricia's going to church with me today. I've made special arrangements about my Sunday school class," she smiled profusely as she spoke to the family.

Once again I felt trapped. I didn't want to disappoint Grandma as I had so many times before by saying no. But did I really want to go with her? No! Trapped! What could I do? I went to my bedroom.

"Patricia, get your Bible it's time to go," Grandma called.

Sparks flew in my head. *How can I get out of this? How can I go to this church house when The Elder said churches are the devil's house and playground? If I go, will the devil laugh and be happy and plan to swallow me in sin? And will God be sad and disappointed if I go to this devil's house? Will I be in the red? Really bad?*

"Patricia, come we're going now," Grandma prodded.

"Go with Grandma," Mom urged as we talked in the bedroom. "You might learn something." *Learn something?* Would this be like going to the dentist? If I obey Mom, was she the one responsible for it being wrong?

My resistance had been wearing down and remembering Fred's comment 'that you'll never know until you try,' I agreed to go to church with Grandma this one time.

I came from the bedroom armed with my Bible in hand

to check this church place out and see if they really teach from the same Bible that I know. Grandma – all smiles – led me to her car, opened the door, and ordered me to sit down! She quickly shut the door, got in on her side, and slammed the door – fast. Did she think I was going to try to escape? She started her old, two-tone green Chevy, and as she backed out, she hit a huge pothole at the end of the drive. Was I going to fall into a pothole like that in the devil's house? I resented the pressure from Grandma forcing me to go with her. What would really happen to me? I didn't understand why she was so sure I'd be blessed at her church. The Elder said I'd be cursed. Who's right and who's wrong?

Clutching my Bible, I followed Grandma as we entered the church. It seemed to me she talked to everybody. We went downstairs to the room where she taught class, and she introduced me to her teaching partner. The lady seemed nice enough. The classes were still in session so we excused ourselves and headed back upstairs.

"We're early," Grandma said. "Let's go find a seat near the back for church." We started into a large room with lots of benches, but instead of finding a seat Grandma kept introducing me to people all over the church. My face turned red at each introduction. People held out their hands to shake. I couldn't shake hands for I was taught that if you shake hands with someone that meant you were in full agreement with them. I wasn't in agreement with any of these strangers. The Elder said hand shaking was strictly forbidden, and I was not about to break one more rule. I kept my hands behind my back. Heart pounding, I felt totally drained before the service even began.

Finally we sat near the back. I watched people stream in like the flocks of birds in the sky coming to our old feeder. So many came the place was nearly packed full and covered with a sea of people. Then a man got up and prayed. "That's the preacher," Grandma whispered.

When he finished, I heard some noise over on one side. There was a big, odd shaped box and a lady was sitting in front of it pounding on black and white pieces of wood to make music.

I had never seen or heard anything like this before. Grandma looked at me and responding to my bewilderment she whispered, "That's a baby grand piano." What did that mean? Was it sinful music? Some of the music sounded kind of nice, but I didn't understand why we needed it. *Oh Lord, please forgive me for being here.*

Rows and rows of people filled the room Grandma called a sanctuary. Where did they all come from? There were so many heads moving and nodding. We always sat absolutely still at our Sabbath meetings.

I jerked at the booming sound of a single voice. A man – not the preacher – talked into a small object. I couldn't tell if it was in his hands or hooked up to something. By this time Grandma realized I didn't understand much of what was going on around me and said, "That's called a microphone."

My hands were clammy, and I had a light headache and 'church' had only been happening for a few minutes. The same questions kept rushing through my mind. Would this take me to hell? What on earth was I doing here? How and why did I get roped into coming into this church? What would The Elder say if he saw me here? Likely he'd give me worse names than my birth name. I believed he would condemn me to hell like he did Mom. Would the Lord tell The Elder I'm here? Well, the Lord saw me. He knew I was here. Instant guilt consumed me. I prayed silently, *"Lord, please forgive me if I'm sinning and keep me from the devil, please."*

Rescuing me from my thoughts, Grandma pulled out a book, "This is a song book, and now we'll sing." *Sing?* I had never sung a note in my life! I wanted so desperately to escape to the security of my bedroom. I was on the edge of panic!

In one hand I gripped my Bible. Grandma held the songbook and pointed to the song on the right-hand page. She began singing as did the people around us. I sat in utter amazement. I watched and listened. It sounded kind of nice, but I didn't know why or how these people could blend their voices together like that. We never had any music or, singing in Lael Colony. The whole experience had me scared. Was it really a sin like The Elder said it was, or was this like the music David wrote about in Psalms? These people were talking about God but was it the same God I knew?

After the first line in the songbook was sung, I was lost. The words they were singing were not on the second line. I knew nothing about music, notes, stanzas, or tunes. Never having seen written music or a songbook before, I was totally confused. I knew nothing of the meaning of the lines with large brackets and backward S's and C's with colons, pound signs, some numbers and alphabets accompanied with funny looking little stems with buds and circles, dots and marks. I starred at the pages. I never opened my mouth to sing or talk.

"All stand," the preacher said.

Grandma stood. *Should I stand like all the other people? Would God condemn me if I did, or if I didn't join would these people condemn me?* Grandma pulled on my clothes lightly urging me up. I stood but wanted to crawl under the seats and hide. Was this really what they call worshiping God? People stared at me. My face burned with embarrassment. I didn't know whether to close my eyes or let them roam as fast as possible. I might never see the inside of another church. Trapped! That's how I felt. I let my eyes, ears, and mind roam waiting for the moment I could flee this place. Fear consumed me. These people sure sang a long time.

I understood only a few words. To my ears they seemed chopped up, dragged out, and slurred. I sat down when Grandma sat.

The preacher said to turn to a Bible chapter and verse. It was a rescue, a moment of reprieve from the strange and unknown. I understood Bible chapters and verses! I quickly opened my worn Bible and found the passage while others – including Grandma – were still searching. I followed every word read. He really did read from the Bible. *How can that be evil?* I wondered.

The preacher began preaching, but I understood very little of what he was saying. I heard words like God, Lord, Jesus Christ, the devil, sin, and evil. But what was he really saying? What is a missionary? And what was that hallelujah word several people kept saying? What does that mean? The preacher shouted – loud, and I trembled. I felt my liver quivering and my heart pounding as the preacher continued slapping that tall stand where he laid his Bible and rested his hands.

The people and the preacher began talking at the same time. I thought it might be praying but it was so loud and confusing. Was that what the Tower of Babel was like in Genesis chapter eleven? Was the devil present here or was it God? I just wanted out! I felt like running!

Grandma sat quietly. She looked at me and whispered, "It's almost over."

A couple of people walked down the aisles. *Where are they going?* I thought. Things got even more confusing as some people mumbled out loud. Others – even Grandma – mumbled in a whisper. How confused could these people get? God's house is to be quiet and orderly and this looked far from orderly to me. It was definitely not quiet!

They sang more songs and then the preacher dismissed the people. The confusion increased for these people acted like swarming bees. They buzzed all around me. Their voices blended. My mind spun in circles.

"Come with me," Grandma ordered.

Where is she going? I wondered. *I hope we're going home!*

"I want you to meet my granddaughter," Grandma said to every person she met.

I burned all over. My face felt red-hot.

"Patricia, meet our preacher," Grandma said. Then she spoke to him, "She doesn't shake hands."

I don't remember saying a word. By this time my eyes hurt and my face felt like red-hot coals.

"Bless you, young lady. God bless you!" the preacher said. "Go in peace."

I felt so far from peace! Was he a servant of the devil as

The Elder always said, or a servant of God as Grandma claimed? He seems nice, but I surely didn't understand much of what he said.

Children rushed and some even ran into me. Amazing! I stood and watched as Grandma visited like she enjoyed all this. Confusion encompassed me and questions flooded my thoughts. Most people left the church as Grandma talked and I waited. Finally Grandma and I walked out the church doors. Once in the car I felt some relief and patiently waited to get home.

I left my first church experience in utter confusion. At the end people talked over each other, and I couldn't make sense of what they said. I didn't know anything about different denominations. But Grandma's church had no meaning for me. I was glad to leave.

"What did you think about church?" Grandma asked on the drive home. "Wasn't it good?"

"I don't know what to think! It surely was different," I said fearing I would disappoint her.

Once home, Grandma went into her bedroom to change clothes and Mom began asking me questions.

"What was Grandma's church like?" Mom persisted.

"It's very confusing!" I replied. People talked over each other. Many were speaking all at once. Do you think that's sinful?"

"I don't know," Mom admitted.

"I know it's confusing for me," I declared.

Every Sunday Grandma continued pleading for me to go again and again. I resisted.

She seemed disappointed and that bothered me, but I had to listen to and follow my own conscience.

Will I ever find a place in this strange world to worship like I was taught by The Elder?

Life seemed hopeless and without an escape.

Patricia Hochstetler

Chapter 13

Learning to Live in Society

Many times I asked myself, "Where will this all end?" From the moment we left the colony change had been continuous. Except for my internal values the *new* was in the process of obliterating what I had known and experienced for the previous 12 years. My very beliefs were being tested and torn from me. I constantly struggled for equilibrium.

The trauma of change seemed unending. My extended family, The Elder, and the colony were gone – forever and for certain – after our trip to Mississippi. My brother, Fred, had forsaken me and gone south. Joan was being weaned on the culture of her environment, and Mom had nothing and no place to call her own. I had no other option than to adjust to this heathen world and its life-style. But I had yet to find a place where I could fit.

I was gaining confidence about my positions in the public workplace. This exposure to people provided acquaintances, but I longed for friends. After my experience at Grandma's church I was positive I couldn't find them there. My social life was nonexistent, and the dismal prospects for that to change added to my discontent with this Indiana world. I was an outsider and not too sure that I wanted in.

The only option for finding friends was finding them on the job. At least I knew where it had to happen, but the 'how' was evasive. I would sometimes change into my 'cult clothes' when I was home. They gave me comfort and allayed a twinge of guilt for my wanderings from The Elder's teachings.

In January, 1965, I was faced with another challenge of

major proportions that would curtail my social growth and adjustment. Dad came to town on a Greyhound bus. He had been released from the Veterans Hospital in Mississippi and sent back home to Indiana.

The first week he was around the house some people he had known years earlier came to see him. I went to the bedroom for refuge, but I listened through the wall. After reminiscing about their past days in Indiana, Dad did most of the talking. He shared about the years we spent in Lael Colony and was interrupted from time to time by their questions. I listened carefully when he began telling about his experiences in the hospital.

Suddenly the topic changed and soon so did the atmosphere.

"You all may not have understood why we left a dozen years ago," Dad stated. I heard sounds of agreement.

"Well, let me explain. I made up my mind that I wanted to get my children out of this wicked environment. I didn't want their minds filled with rubbish or their lives destroyed by the corruption of the world. So I told Mary we had to get to a place where we could live like God intended."

"Now Clarence," a neighbor interjected, "it wasn't that bad 'round here. You had a good job and were doin' real good. We missed you folks all these years, and our kids missed yours. There've been a lot of changes while you were gone."

"That's true," Dad agreed momentarily, "and most of 'em haven't been too good."

The sound of shuffling feet penetrated the stillness. I could feel the tension rising even though I couldn't see the visual exchange among our guests. I couldn't hear everything said by the quiet ones, but I did catch the words school and education. That ignited the firestorm.

"My children might not know much about your world," Dad declared, "but they do know the Bible. I'll show you." *What is he going to do? Is he deliberately trying to start a fight with his old friends?* My thoughts were quickly interrupted.

"Tish," Dad hollered. I froze! *Oh no, these people didn't even know I was in here until now. What can I do to escape this?*

I wanted to jump out the window and run away.

"Tish!" Dad called again and his voice was more forceful. He couldn't use my real name, Patricia, ever since The Elder changed my name back to my birth name. "Tish, come on out here and show these people how you learned the Bible."

With a racing heart, red face, and inwardly trembling, I forced myself to leave the bedroom. The people stared at my colony clothes and head covering. I felt like a freak in a sideshow. I was on stage!

Dad placed a chair beside him where he insisted I should sit. I sat there emotionless. Inside I felt like a volcano about to erupt. I looked at the floor and popped out the answers as fast as Dad asked the questions. I anxiously waited for him to be done and release me to go back to the bedroom. Writing about this more than 35 years later, I can feel the tension rising within me.

"Tish, now tell me the chapter headings for Malachi 2, Genesis 10, Matthew 6, Ezekiel 28, and I Timothy 5," Dad demanded.

I rattled those chapter headings off as fast as he called them out. I was too embarrassed to look at anyone, but I heard their expressions of surprise.

"And what does 2 Timothy 2:15 say?" Dad asked.

What is he trying to do? I wondered. I had no means of escape so I complied. *"Study to shew thyself approved unto God, a workman that needeth not to be ashamed, rightly dividing the word of truth."*

"That's right," someone commented. At least one person knew that verse. *Please, Dad, let that be the last one!*

"Now I'm going to say some chapter headings, and you are to tell what chapter that is in the Bible," Dad ordered. Then he began.

As he gave a chapter heading, I announced where it fit. I'm certain those poor people had no idea if we were right or wrong. We did a few chapters before Dad boasted, "See my children know the Bible and not the wicked things like this world teaches."

These people were not interested in any of this! Why wouldn't Dad let me go?

"Now, Tish, recite Psalm 2:1-12," Dad ordered.

I knew Dad's aim was twofold. He wanted to show off what his child had learned, but he was more anxious to tell these people how wicked they really were. I began to rattle off the chapter. I stumbled over the words in verse five, and Dad stopped me and said, "That's too fast! Stop and start over. Say it a bit slower and speak louder.

How could I do this? I choked inside with all eyes on me as I looked only at the floor. I recited the chapter again.

"Now you can be excused," Dad said.

I rushed to my room sweaty and exhausted. I lay on my bed and listened behind the wall as Dad told his friends what he felt Psalms 2 meant. Beginning with verse one he started a verse by verse explanation.

"Why do the heathens rage and the people imagine a vain thing?" he spoke with deep emotion. I knew he meant that they were all heathens.

The visitors didn't say much and soon left, but my embarrassment lingered. It kept choking me with an iron grip. Why did Dad have to use me? Why didn't he just say the chapter headings and verses himself? He had made me a spectacle! I was churning inside, and it hurt! Didn't he care about my feelings? He knew I couldn't disobey or refuse to answer. I would never be able to face these people again. None of them will ever want their children to be friends with me! This gnawed at me, and I couldn't sleep well for several nights. Whenever I recall the incident, it still gives me a pain in my neck.

Fortunately after his first week in Indiana there were never any other experiences like that. I became reacquainted with Dad on the weekends, but his impact on my social development lasted for several more years.

After Dad got a job and he and Mom could begin planning to buy their own home, tensions eased some. Dad agonized over buying a house and was often upset and growling. His release papers from the Veterans Hospital were accompanied with a prescription, but he refused to take the medicine. Now that he was no longer forced to be hospitalized he followed The Elder's teachings about doctors.

House shopping occupied some of the evenings after they had saved almost enough money to buy their own home and could move out of Grandma's. Meeting people was educational and fun. I was actually becoming more comfortable with these Hoosiers. Maybe I would fit in. God knew I couldn't go back to Lael Colony or even Mississippi.

Chapter 14

The Public Workplace

"If you want a job other than working in cotton fields or baby-sitting you need to get a social security number," Mom urged. "I'll go with you, and I believe Uncle Carl will take us to apply for it. You need it if you want to work in Indiana."

"Why couldn't we have social security numbers in Mississippi? If it was wrong there, why isn't it wrong here in Indiana?" I questioned.

"I don't have all the answers or know much about the nonresistant rules, but that was there and this is here and now," Mom snapped. "I just know you need it to work!"

"Is getting a number like that a part of the mark of the beast that it talks about in the Bible?"

"I don't know," Mom said impatiently. "I had a social security number before we lived in Lael Colony and I asked for mine back and got it! Fred went and got one. Joan doesn't need one to go to school."

"I'll think about it tonight."

I really wanted to keep working at Checkleys Drive-In where Mom worked. I knew I would lose that job if I didn't get a social security number soon. The pressure was on from Mom, Grandma, Uncle Carl, and Mr. Checkley.

I surrendered to the government rules and applied for the number. Was I in danger of hell? Why did Mom and Fred give in to this world? Did she think it didn't matter since The Elder had condemned her to hell already?

I enjoyed working at the restaurant and wanted to keep working even though what they called work was not work

117

compared to what I did in the cotton fields. Yet this job helped me feel useful. Like Fred said, "It's better than doing nothing." I missed him, but I knew it was better for him to have left Indiana before Dad came home. I wondered if he missed Indiana and us. I wanted to tell him all about the new people that Mr. Checkley had hired to replace him and some others.

Susie was one of the new employees I met at Checkley's Drive-In. I learned a lot from her. She was quiet but not shy, and this helped me overcome my reserve and fear of others. I enjoyed the days we worked together. Susie was the first person in my new world to call me her friend and that felt good. She was my first worldly friend.

"I have my driver's license now, and last weekend I bought a black 57 Chevy," Susie said. "Can I take you for a ride?"

"Sure can." I enjoyed the ride.

A few days later she asked,"Tricia, will you come to my home for supper tonight after work and meet my parents and little sister, Valerie?"

"Can you take me home after supper?"

"Yes, you only live two miles from me."

I enjoyed Susie's family. It was a pleasure to share the meal, and I learned from watching how they lived. This was my first experience in any home of someone who wasn't a relative. On the way home Susie had a lot to say, and I listened.

"My family likes you and wants you to go camping with us next weekend. Can you go?"

"I don't know. My parents are very strict. I'll need to ask them, and then I'll let you know." My new world was expanding beyond my family and Lael Colony. I was moving outside my comfort zone.

Not many weeks later Susie found another job at Fair Moore Nursing Home on Hively Avenue in Elkhart and quit Checkley's Drive-In. I missed her at work. After she left I went from washing dishes to garnishing sandwiches and then to the grill.

Susie didn't forget me. Later she called to tell me that the nursing home where she was working wanted to hire and train someone for a nurse's aide. She begged me to apply. Helping people was rewarding for her and she thought I would enjoy it too. I appreciated her thoughtfulness, but I was determined not to change jobs unless I was sure it provided advancement and more money. Mom and I discussed the fact that I would be working in a medical environment with doctors, nurses, patients, and medicines. This was contrary to what The Elder had taught.

In spite of some misgivings I applied at the nursing home and Mrs. Moore hired me to train to become a nurse's aide. I wasn't about to give up the security of my job at Checkley's Drive-In so I kept working there while I took the nurse's aide training. It wasn't long before she hired me for the real job, and I worked the second shift at Fair Moore Nursing Home. Even after I completed the training I continued working days at the drive-in. I was only home long enough to sleep a few hours.

I was impressed when Mrs. Moore gave me a pin with my name on it and two additional words, nurse's aide. I had to buy several white dress uniforms and white shoes. This was another departure from my long, colony clothes.

In my training program I learned how to take patients' blood pressure, pulse, respiration, and temperature. I learned how to bathe and feed them, how to give back rubs, and how to correctly make up a hospital bed. I was responsible for reading and charting 'intake' and 'output' by cc's. I learned how to deal with families of patients. This experience was so different from anything in the cotton fields. Until I became ill, I liked working 40 hours at the nursing home on the second shift and days at the restaurant.

"Patricia, I think you need to see a medical doctor," Mom urged.

"I'll be all right."

"Remember you are to obey your parents. If it's wrong to see a doctor, I'm to blame," Mom assured. "I want you to go see Dr. Classen, Grandma's doctor. Come on! She's out there waiting to take you."

Another first – my first trip to see a medical doctor.

"You have the old fashion measles," Dr. Classen said. "How old are you?"

"Seventeen."

"And you've never had measles before?"

"No!"

"That's unusual at your age. Have you had chicken pox?" Dr. Classen asked.

"No!"

"I hope you don't get them, but if you do come see me."

I felt tired and weak and it was hard for me to keep up with two jobs. I eventually quit the restaurant.

Susie and I liked working together as nurse's aides. We enjoyed helping the elderly people, and they seemed to like us. I can vividly recall a 95 year old lady that everybody called granny or Grandma Elliot. She was very small, had a clear complexion, and couldn't talk, but her piercing blue eyes and expressions told it all. "Grandma Elliot, would you like to sit up and powder your face?" I asked.

Delight spread across her face. She nodded yes.

Ten to fifteen minutes later, "Granny, are you tired?"

Her head dropped and a soft, smooth sigh signaled that she was tired and ready for a rest.

Knowing Sandy, a 29-year-old lady, was a heartbreaking experience. She had been in an accident on her honeymoon and was left comatose and tube-fed. "Good morning, Sandy, how are you?" I asked daily.

Occasionally she groaned, and there were moments that she smiled. I carefully brushed her teeth, combed her hair, and bathed her. Sometimes I could tell when she liked something. I talked to her and wondered if she understood what I said. I wished she would awaken and talk and surprise everybody. She never did.

Mrs. Long, an Alzheimer patient at age 49, wandered around the halls daily. "What are you doing?" she would ask and interrupt anyone in the area. Without waiting for an answer she would announce, "I'm looking for my coat and can't find it. I want to go to town. Will you help me?"

"Yes, but this isn't your room. We need to go to your room to find your coat," I coaxed. "Would you like to work on a puzzle?"

By the time I took the poor soul back to her room she had forgotten what she wanted.

These were just a few of the fifteen patients I helped daily. This was my classroom and these patients were my teachers. Another patient, Mrs. Beesley, taught me about confrontation. She talked to herself much like my Dad did and she, too, was always miserable and seemed to make everyone else miserable too.

"Come, come, I need you," Mrs. Beesley squealed. "There are some funny sounds in the closet. Get them out of here right now!"

"I'll take care of it," I declared and opened and closed the closet door. That satisfied her for the moment. Before I could get to the hallway, she would comment, "Since you're here, will you put lotion on my back and give me one of your good back rubs?" Mrs. Beesley was a master of manipulation. She refused to take 'no' for an answer.

I was familiar with a demanding adult voice, and it was hard not to respond to her wishes. Time and job activities forced me to learn to deal with her demands and develop positive ways to deal with her confrontation.

Every patient had their own set of problems. For many there was only one resolve as their life wasted away. I knew they were destined to return to ashes, but in the meantime they all needed our help each day.

I learned much more in nursing than at the restaurant. Every night was like a new class with challenging learning experiences. I listened carefully to the patients, RN's, and other aides. They had all become my teachers.

I became quite comfortable working for Mrs. Moore, a lady like some of the conservative Mennonite women I had met in Mississippi. I never asked her any questions about her past because I didn't want her asking about mine. I also liked Mrs. Moore's daughter, Sharon, a college student majoring in nursing. I worked with her one summer. Later Mrs. Moore called me into her office and pleaded with me to go to nursing school to become a registered nurse. She even offered to help pay my tuition. I feared that if I did she would discover my past, so I told her no.

Susie had a steady boyfriend and talked about dating, the places they went, and what they did. This was an education that I wasn't ready to tap into. I was all ears listening to her every word and stored up a lot of information for later. Susie knew my Dad was strict and had forbidden me to date until I was eighteen. She knew nothing of my Amish-Jewish background. When she asked about school, I told her that I had attended a small private school down in Mississippi and she never questioned me.

Work was not the same without Susie when she moved on to another job. I began to feel additional pressure to please Mrs. Moore and go to nursing school. I still enjoyed caring for my patients but pondered if I really wanted to stay in nursing. It was during this period that Kinders Manufacturing, where Mom worked, began hiring. They paid more than I made at the nursing home. I applied and they hired me. Mrs. Moore pleaded with me not to quit so I worked the two jobs for a few months. I didn't really want to quit but I also liked sewing mattress covers at Kinders and working near Mom.

After six months working two jobs became too much. I was tired all the time. Sharon Moore had quit her summer job at the nursing home to go back to college. I missed Sharon and many of my patients had died. Eventually I realized that quitting my job at the nursing home was my best option. It was at Kinder's that I met Judy Stiver who became a great influence in my life.

Occasionally I went back to the nursing home to visit some of my patients and Mrs. Moore. After several who were very dear to me died, I visited less often and eventually decided to quit going.

I continued trying to maintain my Lael Colony religious rituals. I liked studying the Bible in my own small bedroom, and I tried to keep Saturday as my Sabbath the best I could. That routine was altered when I was asked to work Saturdays. I had to either show up on Saturdays or lose my job at Kinders. I couldn't chance that, so with great reluctance I agreed just like Mom had done earlier. I still kept the dietary laws and so did Mom and Dad. Life was beginning to feel more tolerable.

By that time I had my driver's license, but Mom and I still walked to work. I enjoyed the freedom that driving gave me on the weekends, and Joan enjoyed it too. She had turned 17 and had a hard time with her school activities and quit. I drove when Joan and I went roller skating at Eby Pines on Sunday afternoons. We even began going on Saturdays, our former Sabbath.

By now I had lived two years in my new world. When ever possible I still tried to keep Saturday as my Sabbath and read the Bible and rehearsed chapters and verses I had learned in the colony. I had stopped reading the Bible during the week when I worked two full time jobs. Sometimes on my jobs I rehearsed verses and chapters, but I began spending more time with people.

I heard that Chicago Telephone Supplies—CTS—was hiring. That was *the* place to work. It was the top-paying job in northern Indiana. I liked my job at Kinders, but I was always looking for ways to advance – intellectually, financially, and socially. I was now resigned to living in Indiana and wanted to learn everything I could so I would fit in and be a part of this world.

I never expected to leave Kinders, but one day I had the chance to interview for a job at CTS and I made the appointment. It was a rigorous interview and I had to tell about my experiences in the private one room school. The fact that the Bible was the main subject was not an obstacle since I had studied typing. Jerry Ash hired me. I was elated! Many college educated people worked in this place because they received higher pay than teaching and other professional careers.

CTS was a new classroom and I was an eager student.

I was enrolled in "Society and People 101." This was my fourth job and I felt I had reached the top of the workplace ladder. I could do no better. I soon was taking home $100 a week.

Most of the time I remained quiet and listened to the conversation of others. I had no urge to say more than I needed to. I didn't have enough life experiences to share, and I was not eager to share those I did have. I had shut the door—tight—to the colony rules. I did not want to reopen it because it was too confusing. I was beginning to feel more and more thankful with what God had provided for me and wanted to go on with life.

The good, the bad, and the ugly were all present at CTS just like every place. Much of what I heard sounded like Greek to me. People talked about songs they knew, television programs they watched, food, cars, government, and the list went on. I was discovering just how big a gap did exist in my life from the 50's and early 60's. My life experiences included no context for holidays, celebrations, songs, games, or nursery rhymes. I was trying to cram the 12 years of disconnected happenings which took place while I was in the isolation of Lael Colony into a few months on the job in Elkhart.

Conversations were sometimes meaningless. I had no understanding of advertising, card games, or traveling. People asked why I was so serious. "Do I look that serious?" was my response. Then I realized I really was serious! I had lived 12 years in total isolation without play, song, or laughter. All those everyday things which were a part of everyone else's lives never existed for me. Those things that others took for granted were completely unknown to me.

Fortunately God had some special people willing to mentor me even though they were unaware of it. Rita and Shirley Minegar were two of these special people. At 18 I became open to guidance. Shirley was rather quiet but forceful when necessary. She had a religious background and I could identify with that. She talked a lot about her church and her family. I liked to listen to her words of wisdom. Little did she know she had served as one of the great teachers in life until more than thirty years later when I told her I was writing this book.

Sharon Gentzhorn Clark decided I needed to date, and she set up a blind date for me. Sharon and her husband and 'John' and I had a dinner date. She always had plenty to say and created lots of excitement. That was my introduction to dating.

There were countless people at CTS that I fondly recall as my teachers in one way or another. Some I wanted to follow in their footsteps. From others I learned by walking beside them and learned from their mistakes.

The workplace was my classroom. My on-the-job colleagues were my teachers. Time was the healer, and Lael Colony was fading into the past. But I was lonely. My heart-cry for God had not lessened, but I was far less certain of where to find Him. Nevertheless I was determined to accomplish two things. I would follow God with all my heart, and I would learn how to cope in this new world — my world.

Patricia Hochstetler

Chapter 15

Deliverance

Progress is always appreciated, but it never assures victory. I could review the changes and gains during the last two years, but my joy was tempered by the realization of the journey ahead. The forced separation from Lael Colony was traumatic, but it faded into nothingness when compared with the ordeal of adjusting to an environment not only foreign to the colony but down-right antagonistic to much of what I was taught to believe.

It was true I was adjusting to Hoosier values and customs, but I had little peace. There was the continual struggle over spiritual issues. It was impossible to exist in the two worlds of ideas, values, and truth without constantly questioning every detail. At least I was beginning to enjoy a meager degree of self-reliance. Truth was hidden somewhere between the extremes of Lael Colony and Elkhart, Indiana. I had to find them!

I had a job, a room in our family home, a car, a small measure of independence, but inner peace was illusive. Friends were bridges to my choices. My personality—my history—required that I come to terms with my spiritual values before I could ever be at rest. Having had 12 years of brainwashing and dictatorial leadership, I was on guard when anyone insisted they had *the* answer.

Three people were especially involved in my spiritual search. Judy and Barbara Stiver and Rita Boren were workplace friends. But they were more. They included me in their families' gatherings and social activities. I was invited for dinner, to visit, to go along to concerts, and to join them on camping trips, to be a part of their world. Church was also an important part of their lives, and I soon went to church with them too.

When I went with them, I found freedom to sit and listen and watch how things were done. I was not forced into anything by anybody. That felt good. This church experience was totally different than any I had before. Here for the first time I began to grasp the full meaning of God's love. The power of John 3:16 gripped me. *"For God so loved the world that he gave his only begotten son that whosoever believeth in him should not perish but have everlasting life."* The words were not new, but the quiet presence of the Holy Spirit was new as He revealed that God's gift is never earned. Jesus Christ's death on the cross paid the price of our eternal salvation.

This was totally unlike any presentation of The Elder's lectures. It was not the mixed and confusing sounds of Grandma's church. I was too frightened and unprepared to fit in. For some reason that didn't matter here. Every church has its rituals, and I wanted to know about how others worshipped. There were so many things I had to learn — like music. I didn't know how to sing, so I would only listen. Acceptance of change was a process, and I had to grow in acceptance.

I became more comfortable just sitting in the church building, listening to others worship, and watching their every move. I learned that the church was not the house of the devil or his playground, unlike what The Elder had taught Nor would a curse be placed on me for entering a church. This church was truly a house of God and full of people who tried their best to do what God says and the Bible teaches.

The church atmosphere and the people appealed to me. Even though I didn't understand everything, I was willing to discover more of what the Bible really teaches. I was finally admitting that I was really ready to question what I had been taught and had totally accepted before. Where and when would I find deliverance from my quagmire of confusion? Where and when would I finally find God's truth?

I had crossed a line. I was ready – not to ignore what I had been taught – but ready to open my mind to see what the Bible really says. I wanted to explore, to compare, and to make my own decisions – totally! It was a liberating step.

I came to the realization that I could not use my mom, dad, or grandma or relatives in the cult as a crutch. They were no longer valid excuses for who I was or what I believed. Why I felt like a total world misfit was not their fault. I searched my soul deep and wide. Confusion began to clear as the fog slowly lifted. My past was history and I couldn't change it. Where do I begin?

I needed to start my life over and learn from scratch. Something was flawed with my past. Yet there was some good, and I didn't want at that moment to decide what was or wasn't. I would have to pick and chose what to keep from my childhood, what to let go of, and what to store for future use. I had to shut the door to my past and not look back until I could find stabilization. Looking back was too confusing. It created guilt. It raised questions too numerous to mention or deal with. It had been a long painful journey from Mississippi to Indiana – from Lael Colony to Elkhart.

I wanted to learn to live in my new world and be productive. I wanted to have value for somebody or something. I was determined to use my past stumbling blocks as stepping stones to my future. I was prepared to settle for one step at a time. I knew education was the door to positive change.

I needed a foundation to build on. I had to know the way to live that was right and pleasing to God. What about all the traditions, feasts and fasts, dos and don'ts that I had been taught? They were all I knew. Should I trash my head covering, long heavy clothes, keeping of the Sabbaths and the Day of Atonement, dietary laws, not to shake hands or touch money, and so much more? Those things walked over and over in my mind. Yet I knew if I was to survive in this new world, I had to make a concrete decision and not waver.

I was on a search for God's truth – God's way. I remembered the Bible verse, *"I am the way, the truth, and the life."* That's what I wanted — truth and life! I remembered my day of reckoning when I was nine. It had been so real! It still is. I promised God that day that I would never forsake Him. I knew if I was going to find truth and life I had to start within myself and grow as a newborn baby.

In my search I began to feel a pull or need to go to church regularly and be with what seemed like God's people — people trying to serve Him. I had so many questions, and the only way to find answers was to go see and search for myself. This brought me to the point of self-examination. My friends did not force me, but I found myself wanting to be more like them, stable people with inner peace.

In this church I heard scripture read, explained, and discussed. Many of the same verses that I had read and memorized now took on a new meaning where before they were just good words. Now it was different. I began to understand God's Word, and it was no longer just words to read and say daily.

I found new hope when a pastor questioned me as to what I believed. He asked me a series of questions which I could answer easily.

"Do you believe in God?"

"Oh yes, for as long as I can remember."

"Do you believe the Bible is true?"

"Of course I believe that."

"Do you believe in God as the one and only master of the universe?

"Yes, of course." I wasn't sure this was helping me in my search.

He opened his Bible and pointed out to me what the Bible plainly teaches.

"Here is what it teaches about sin," he said as he opened his Bible. "In Romans 3:23 we read these words: *All have sinned and come short of the glory of God.* That includes you and me."

I nodded for I had read that verse before.

"Everybody needs to pray and ask God for forgiveness," the pastor continued. "The Bible says that God is faithful and just to forgive everyone who asks Him. If we do, God will wash our sins away, and we will be as white as snow."

He turned a few pages in his Bible.

"Here is what Romans 6:23 has to say. *For the wages of sin is death: but the gift of God is eternal life through Jesus Christ our Lord.* This means that God is offering us a free gift and all we need to do is receive it. Salvation is a free gift for the asking!"

I sat quietly absorbing all the pastor had said.

"Patricia, Romans 5:8 has a wonderful statement about God's love. It says *God commends his love toward us, in that, while we were yet sinners, Christ died for us."*

Once more he turned a few pages in the book of Romans. "Now let's see what Romans 10: 9-10 promises."

I followed along as he pointed to the words and read them aloud.

"Romans 10:9-10 promises — *If thou shalt confess with thy mouth the Lord Jesus, and shalt believe in thine heart that God hath raised him from the dead, thou shalt be saved. For with the heart man believeth unto righteousness: and with the mouth confession is made unto salvation.*

"According to the Bible, which you believe is true, you need to ask God's forgiveness and ask Him to save you. The Bible says that He is faithful and just and will save you if you ask Him to. God didn't say you might or maybe you would be saved. He said, 'you will be saved' if you ask. Do you believe that?" the pastor asked.

"Yes, I believe it. But it's never been pointed out to me before. I never heard anything like this."

Quietly the pastor spoke, "If you believe this is true, why don't you bow your head now and ask God to forgive you and ask Him to come into your heart and be your personal Savior?"

It seemed so simple. It was so different from what I'd been taught. The pastor didn't say one word about keeping dietary laws or observing the Sabbath or all the do's and don'ts I'd known about all my life. He was talking about what God wanted to do for me. That seemed like the right thing to do.

I looked into the pastor's face. "I want to do what you said."

As he prayed, I repeated each phrase after him.

"Lord, I confess that I am a sinner. Please forgive all my sins. I invite you to come into my heart to be my personal savior now. In Jesus name I pray. Amen."

That was it.

"I witnessed your confession unto salvation, Patricia," the pastor stated. "Now according to the Bible you are a child of God. He has adopted you into his family, and you are His child. He will care for you. You are like a babe in Christ. Now grow in Him. Go learn more about God and He will bless you."

There was nothing to say. There was a calm, a sense of peace.

"Now that you asked God to save you, you might want to make a public confession of your faith in God and go forward in church. That has nothing to do with your salvation, but it announces to the people that you intend to follow God. After that if you want to show that you have a desire to follow in Christ's footsteps, I'll baptize you." the pastor said. "And it's up to you if you want to become a member of our church."

I knew the answers to the pastor's questions, but I wanted some time to assimilate all this new teaching. There was still a lot that I couldn't understand all at once. I had taken a step of faith and before long I followed the Lord in baptism.

At that moment in my life I found hope for living now and the promise of eternal life through Jesus Christ's love, mercy, and grace. Hope had always been available for me, and at last I found it! Deliverance!

Instead of anger I found love.

Instead of warfare I found peace.

Instead of rejection I found acceptance.

In the midst of my struggles I found rest.

In the depth of my despair I found hope.

Deliverance

Instead of surviving by works I found salvation by grace – God's grace.

From delusion and deception I found deliverance through Jesus Christ.

Patricia Hochstetler

Epilogue

With most of the pain of my cult life behind me I can now take a better look at the overall picture and see how it all played out according to God's plan. In my darkest moments He was with me and carried me through my shattered hope. He directed my path in this new world. It was He who guided me in self-examination.

As difficult as it has been to go back and open those tightly closed doors and spade up that hard ground of cult living, it is my prayer that anyone who reads this book will find hope. Regardless of what has happened, God is able to deliver from the pain and heartache. By God's mercy He spared my life. God stood with me, protected me, delivered me, and gave me freedom through Him.

Culture shock is not exclusively a third world phenomenon. It happens in the United States. Like a homing pigeon it is natural to want to return to the known even when the unknown may be far better. Facing the unknown is when you learn how much you really trust God or how willing you are to trust Him. It's in the times of uncertainty that you discover the strength of His everlasting arms.

I thank God for deliverance, for guiding my footsteps, and leading me to an emotional, physical and spiritual healing according to His will and on His schedule. The sunlight now is brighter because I have lived in the shadows. Even beautiful sunsets are harbingers of the darkness of night, but joy comes in the morning with the sunrise of opportunity for a new day.

I know there will be other storms. But God's deliverance from the stranglehold of misguided teachers assures me that He will never leave me hopeless and alone.

We have only one chance at life and it is extremely important to enjoy our path on this earthly journey and to make the most we can of our life as God intended and desires for us. Not only did He close the doors to what I wanted, He showed me better turf and led me to His love and saving grace.

God is willing to do the same for you!

To contact Patricia Hochstetler, the author of the trilogy
Growing Up in an Amish-Jewish Cult
write, email or check her website:

Patricia's Books
P.O. Box 1071
Goshen, IN 46527

E-mail: info@amishjewishcult.com
Website: www.amisihjewishcult.com

Other Books by Patricia Hochstetler

Patricia's series of poetry books
Sunrises - December 2007
Sunrays - May 2008
Sunsets - November 2008

Book One
Delusion

The story of one child, Patricia Hochstetler, caught in the trap of parental good intentions. Between the ages of four and six she was snatched from the warmth of *Jesus Loves Me* and thrust into a world that was cold and barren.

She wanted to please God and her parents, but the harder she tried the more desperate and confused she became. "Why is my aunt hiding out in the woods? Why did my cousin get taken out and dumped? Why is my father acting so strange? What can I do to be sure I'm going to heaven?" These questions could never be answered for no one dared question the rules.

The author reminds us that no one decides to join a *cult*. Parents set out to find truth, to draw closer to God. In their wayward search their children become scarred. Confusion reigns because the rules change for no apparent reason. If it was good yesterday, why is it bad today?

We see how the trap was set for one little girl and her family. Her memories and family stories reveal how powerful the need to belong really is. It is a revelation of how much they were willing to surrender in order to be a part of the group. These people were industrious, intelligent, compassionate, and God-fearing. But the lack of discernment brought broken relationships, heartache, despair, and even death.

Patricia Hochstetler

Book Two

Deception

Growing Up
in an
Amish-Jewish Cult

Book Two
Deception

This book continues our dark journey into the life of a young girl totally isolated from any world beyond a small Tennessee valley and the vast cotton fields of a Mississippi plantation. We find her Garden of Eden turned into a prison camp of child labor and captured souls. We encounter The Elder's burdensome rules and messages he claimed to bring directly from God, only to strangle the humanity of every follower. The joys of paradise have gradually metamorphosed into the pains of an earthly hell. Still they hoped for salvation.

How can such good people who are committed to Christ find themselves so helplessly lost in another man's egocentric nightmare? How can parents bear to watch their children suffer and even die and still show no emotion? How can a child born in a Christian home live 12 years of her childhood without ever hearing "I love you" cross the lips of her parents, family, or church? How could she go through her childhood and never hear music? Was this really what these good parents set out to give their children? NO!

They set out to give their children the assurance of God's salvation through Jesus Christ. They set out to surround their children with the *love* and support of a cohesive Christian community. They set out to assure their children of the reality of God's *love*.